THE

PHANTOM RAPIST

From one cop to another

Timothy C. Richards

2014 Timothy C. Richards, Author.
All rights reserved
ISBN 9781-5052-83686

Published by Xznark Press LLC   St. Louis, Mo. 63129
xznark.com
$19.95

Tim Richards

THE
Phantom
Rapist

Copyright © 2014 Tim Richards

ISBN: 9781-5052-83686

All rights reserved. No part of this book may be reproduced in any form or by any electronic or mechanical means, including information storage or retrieval systems, without permission in writing from the publisher, except by a reviewer, who may quote brief passages in review.

Printed in the United States of America

ACKNOWLEDGMENTS

There are a number of people I would like to express my gratitude to in the writing of this book. I did extensive research at the Mercantile Library at the University of Missouri, St. Louis, and obtained just about everything they had to offer on the serial rapist Patrolman Milton Brookins.

The Intelligence Unit of the St. Louis Metropolitan Police Department has a file on Milton Brookins. After spending 8 years as a detective in that unit, and 35 years as a dedicated police officer in the St. Louis Metropolitan Police Department, I was not allowed to view Patrolman Milton Brookins file.

In my research, I would come across a police officer's name who worked on the ancient case. I telephoned the pension office, hoping to make contact with one of the old cops who worked the case. Most were deceased.

I interviewed retired Detective Sergeant Ron Adler, and he gave me some information.

My big break came when Detective George Hotsenpiller, a name I had gleaned during my research, was contacted by the pension office, and called me back.

The pension office will not give a pensioner's telephone number to a caller requesting it, even if the caller is also a retired cop.

A pension representative telephones the cop and advises him that another retired cop is attempting to get in touch with him, and gives him, or her, your telephone number. Sometimes they call you back---sometimes they don't.

Detective George Hotsenpiller called me back. I advised him that I was writing a book about serial rapist, Patrolman Milton Brookins, AKA, the Phantom Rapist, and that I'd like to meet with him and pick his brain. I knew from my research that he was the lead detective on the case.

We had a brief telephone conversation—we didn't know one another, and had never, even briefly, met. Finally Detective Hotsenpiller said, "I have the file on the case, police reports, and photos. You can have it if you want it."

I rushed to Union, Missouri, met with George and obtained the file. I asked him why he kept the file all of these years. "I don't know," he replied. "It was an interesting case, probably the most interesting case I ever worked on. I just wanted my son to have it someday."

Without George's help, there would not have been a book on Milton Brookins.

My friend, police academy cohort, and ninth district riding partner, Patrolman William Robinson, greatly helped me with much of the inside information on Patrolman Milton Brookins.

Little did I know that forty years after our long, night watch conversations, I would become a "true crime" writer and remember his descriptive information on Milton Brookins. William Robinson is one of the few people who actually knew Milton.

I am indebted to the descendants of Acting Sergeant Harry Freeman, DSN 0697, who proudly, and unselfishly, served the City of St. Louis from 1945 to 1974.

Guys like Harry Freeman are the backbone of the police department. He was never recognized for his loyalty to the City of St. Louis, but that did not deter him from doing an honest and remarkable job.

I'd like to acknowledge my friend and proof reader, Kathy Grove. Kathy is a retired English teacher, and the wife of a retired police sergeant. She never turns me down when I'm in need of structure, punctuation, or paragraph content.

Kathy helps me because she is a kind and caring person. She took an interest in my first nonfiction book, "Crooks

Kill, Cops Lie", and has helped me from day one on all of published work.

To my friend Thomas Noftsinger, my computer guru who is always there to help me when I screw something up. Without Tom, this book, and my other books would not be a reality.

To my wife Carrie, the person who strokes my balding head, and assures me everything is going to be alright, after a tough day of writing, and an even tougher day of selling.

And to my police department librarian friend, Barbara Miksicek who always tells me, "The book's good Tim, it's really good."

AUTHOR'S NOTE

This is a work of nonfiction. My research materials included police reports, news archives, interviews, and some victim statement material.

The names of the rape victims were omitted from this book, but the locations are true and accurate. The dates and time are also accurate, as well as the descriptive details of the rapes, assaults, and robberies.

I have endeavored to maintain the factual and quintessential integrity of both the people and the events related herein.

1

After the Great Civil War, and at the beginning of the Reconstruction Period of America, hundreds of thousands of southern slaves, now free men and women, and American Citizens, sought to leave the south for cities in the North.

They descended upon Washington, D.C. en masse, demanding that the United States Government feed and clothe them, and give them housing and employment.

It was the beginning of the entitlement movement in America, and it has never slowed or stopped, even when conservative politics attempted to dissolve it.

The City of St. Louis, Missouri was sympathetic with the Underground Railroad movement that moved escaped slaves from the south into St. Louis and nearby Alton, Illinois.

President Lincoln signed the Emancipation Proclamation freeing all slaves in 1863, but there were states that were omitted from the law of freedom for slaves. They were referred to as slave states and Missouri was one of them.

Prior to the signing of the Emancipation Proclamation, in 1861, the Governor of the Great State of Missouri, Claiborne Fox Jackson created a special state convention in an attempt to take Missouri into the Confederacy. The Union Army chased Jackson and his like-minded legislators out of Jefferson City.

In Jackson's absence, the convention made Hamilton Gamble, a Virginia lawyer, the provisional governor. He was a Unionist who backed slavery.

St. Louis was filled with refugees from the guerrilla war raging in the state. Governor Gamble died in 1864 and Charles Drake, a lawyer and a Radical Republican, named because of their loathing of slavery, took office. In reality, Drake had at one time supported slavery.

On January 11, 1865, Missouri's slaves were given freedom. Celebrating crowds of blacks jammed the streets of downtown St. Louis. They felt they had gained freedom and equality in the land of the free and that the "white devil" would accept them as equals.

Thousands of freed slaves travelled to the City of St. Louis, seeking jobs, housing, food, and education for their children. They squatted in an area known as Mill Creek, or Mill Valley, just west of the prosperous downtown business district, bounded by Olive, Chestnut, North Jefferson, and North 22nd Street, near the historical Union Station Train Depot.

They built themselves a small city, complete with grocery, hardware and clothing stores, restaurants, schools and churches, all within walking distance of their homes.

Mill Creek Valley housed 20,000 inhabitants, (95% African-American) and included over 800 businesses and institutions.

In reality Mill Creek was an open sewer, with a gigantic sewer pipe buried beside it carrying sewage from the west part of the metropolitan area to the Mississippi River. Most of the homes and businesses had outhouses, and some didn't have running water.

In 1892 there was a sewer gas explosion in the sewer pipe in Mill Creek Valley that leveled blocks of shanties, killing several people. The explosion opened up the earth, and housing, people, tracks, and trains were swallowed up. The shanty dwellings were rebuilt.

The city fathers saw Mill Creek Valley as a slum. They didn't take into consideration that in actuality it was a functioning neighborhood within the boundaries of the City of St. Louis. It was a city within a city, and a cultural phenomenon.

Generations of poor freed slaves raised their families

there. It was once the home of such famous African-Americans as Scott Joplin and Josephine Baker. The St. Louis Argus newspaper was founded there. Mill Creek Valley was a closed culture. Blacks tended to remain inside of their closed society. Whites very seldom ventured into Mill Creek Valley.

The older blacks, the ones not far removed from slavery, schooled the younger generations of the horrors of slavery and the evil of the "white devil".

In Illinois, on the east side of the Mississippi River, a ferry boat landing called Illinois Town had sprung up. The land was flat and easily built upon. Railways flocked to the location and so did industry. The Eads Bridge was built, connecting the thriving City of St. Louis, Missouri to the ferry landing, Illinois Town. The name was quickly changed to East St. Louis, Illinois.

The housing in East St. Louis, Illinois was drab and cheap, not like the brick structures in St. Louis, Missouri. The East Side structures were made of wood and clapboard and mostly were flat on the moist soil.

Southern blacks flocked to East St. Louis seeking employment in the National Stockyards, the Aluminum Ore Company, American Steel Foundry, Republic Iron and Steel, Obear-Nester Glass, and Elliot Frog and Switch.

World War 1 came about and everyone in East St. Louis who desired employment got work. The best place to work was at the Aluminum Ore Company. It paid the most and they treated their employees better than the other industries.

In 1917 there was a strike at the Aluminum Ore Company. The owners of the company fired the striking workers and hired immigrant southern blacks to take their place.

Embittered white union strikers complained to their union leaders. The union leaders went to City Hall and demanded that the city get rid of the black southern migrants.

On July 1st, white men in a black Ford shot into some blacks' homes. Black groups gathered at tenth and Bond Avenue and shot into a black Ford, killing the two occupants; they were East St. Louis, Illinois police detectives who were dispatched to the scene to investigate the shooting into the dwellings of the blacks.

The next morning rampaging white mobs began beating and killing any black they could find. Blacks were hanged from light standards, shot and beaten, and their homes were set on fire. The official body toll was thirty nine blacks and nine whites killed; the unofficial toll was in the hundreds on each side.

Thousands of East St. Louis blacks fled to St. Louis---walked across the Eads Bridge, and were given refuge by the City of St. Louis. They were given temporary housing, money and food, and subsequently made their way to the Mill Creek Valley neighborhood.

The East St. Louis, Illinois race riot was just another incident for the black inhabitants of Mill Creek Valley to lecture their young about. The "white devil" was the enemy of the black race, and every young black person was raised on stories of black oppression, murder and slavery.

The inhabitants lived a subsistence existence with poor education, meager employment, and sub-standard housing, living hand to mouth for a hundred years.

Under the 1954 Federal Housing Act which provided federal aid for renewal projects, and the passage in 1955 of a $110 million bond issue, Mayor Tucker and the City of St. Louis began the clearance and demolition of slums in Mill Creek Valley.

By spring of 1959 Mill Creek Valley was cleared. The displaced residents were given the opportunity to move into high rise housing projects around the city. Many took the government up on their offer.

A large contingent of Mill Creek Valley residents didn't want to partake of the government offer of high rise housing. They desired homes. They went to the neighborhood bank, Jefferson Bank and Trust, on Jefferson just north of the old Mill Valley slums. They were rejected for home loans, partially due to the low pay from their menial jobs.

Some were lucky to find employment in the downtown area, but those jobs were janitorial or service jobs in the retail market. There were no good jobs for slum dwelling blacks. Union jobs went to whites and relatives of local politicians. There was no good future for the blacks of St. Louis, Missouri.

In 1963 the St. Louis African-American community began to produce leaders. In August of that year 150 blacks, led by Norman Seay (educator, who later became the Administrator for the University of Missouri—St. Louis) and William Lacy Clay (alderman who later became a United States Congressman) led a civil disobedience movement at Jefferson Bank.

They demanded economic equality, access to fair home loans, and they demanded that the bank hire black people. They locked arms and blocked the bank entrance, and ignored a court order against such demonstrations.

Eventually nineteen of the demonstrators spent sixty days in jail for the disturbance. The Jefferson Bank hired five black clerical workers.

But banking institutions weren't the only culprits. There were very few blacks on the St. Louis Metropolitan Police Department. Most didn't desire the job. They had been indoctrinated that the cop was their natural enemy, the enforcement arm of the "white devil."

Ghetto blacks becoming big-city cops was akin to a Jew joining the American Nazi Party. But some joined. The job provided acceptance into the white establishment, something few slum dwellers had ever experienced in the City of St. Louis, Missouri. It was a steady paycheck, and the job had some power.

The cop could get his friends' and relatives' traffic citations "fixed". The black cop was immune from petty racial profiling from the district cops, and with the flash of the badge the cop could get a discount on almost anything. On the street you were "the man".

Very few St. Louis blacks had ever had the feeling of belonging to the establishment. Many joined just to take advantage of the educational benefits offered by the city. Most didn't stay in the field of endeavor. Their culture moved them on.

To say the police department was racist is an understatement. Cops are equal opportunity haters. Most of the white cops hate everybody, no matter their race. Most of the black cops are the same.

Street justice prevailed within the St. Louis Metropolitan Police Department. The cop on the street was the judge, and the jury. The nightstick and the pistol were the means of punishment.

The Circuit Attorney's office seldom issued warrants on street justice cases. In the mind of the establishment, the cop did his job and there was no further need for prosecution or punishment. This mindset was accepted by everyone, even the slum dwelling blacks.

When I interviewed for the cop job at the St. Louis Metropolitan Police Department in the late 60's, I went before a panel of high ranking cops, all white.

It was a casual conversation between them and me. Eventually one of the high ranking guys asked me, "How are you going to feel if you have to ride in a police car for eight hours with a Negro patrolman?"

I wasn't quick to answer. The question was ignorant. The panel had my employment records before them. We had discussed my four years in the United States Marine Corps. Did he think I didn't live with black Marines? It dawned on me that he knew the answer before he asked the question. He was, in his own ignorant way, setting the tone of the police department for me. It was the beginning of the indoctrination process from crazy Marine to big-city-cop. He was actually saying, "You got to be a hater to be in this job, can you do it?"

As time progressed and I was riding in a beat car in the bloody ninth district, I had a black female partner. When a cop has a riding partner most of the shift consists of talking about our individual lives, past, present, and future. The cop partners know each other almost as well as relatives. We even refer to one another as "cousin."

As I rode with this black lady cop there was no communication between us. She wouldn't talk to me. I asked her if anything was wrong. She said "no." I asked her why she wouldn't talk to me. She told me she had never been around white people, and she had never been in a car with a white man. She had lived in St. Louis for her entire life.

Even wealthy African-Americans had to tread lightly when trying to purchase a home in the good neighborhoods. Doctor Leslie Bond, a St. Louis surgeon wanted to buy some land on Lindell Boulevard across from Forest Park. He didn't use his real name. He used the name of a relative who didn't have a birth certificate, to make it difficult for anyone to track down the race of the buyer.

Many neighborhoods were segregated, and the residents wanted to keep them that way. Doctor Bond's ploy worked.

He purchased the land and built a home. He later was appointed to the St. Louis Board of Police Commissioners by the Governor of the State of Missouri.

After demolition of the Mill Creek Valley, land was partially gobbled up by St. Louis University, Harris Stowe Teachers College, and several railroads. There was still some land available to the Federal Government.

The U.S Department of Housing and Urban Development decided to build an experimental housing complex on land west of downtown, north of Laclede, and partially connected to St. Louis University land to the west. The government was going to create from scratch an integrated, mixed-income small neighborhood.

Potential residents were hand-picked, and some of the units were reserved for St. Louis University students. HUD planned a mix of public and private investment, and hired a big-time architect, Chloethiel Woodard Smith, and gave it a radical plan, different than anything the government had ever built before.

It was called Laclede Town, a traditional neighborhood, bright and colorful with a few blocks of streets lined with St. Louis style row houses.

It had a town circle, a coffee house café with outside tables, buildings with small shops facing the street and apartments above. Laclede Town was new urbanism, 30 years ahead of its time. It was in full swing in the mid 60's.

Laclede Town was cool and hip. It was cheap and populated by people who bet the farm on making integration of the races a successful reality.

The complex was made up of two components. Laclede Park was privately funded and rented apartments at market rates. Across the intersection of Laclede and Compton was Laclede Town.

It was a community of federally funded townhouses.

Rent was based on family size and income. It brought together a community of people, black, white, brown, Jews, Christians, Muslims and atheists. There were lawyers, architects, sanitation workers, actors, athletes, draft dodgers, hookers, social workers, welfare recipients, musicians, reporters, waiters, politicians, doctors and a St. Louis City cop named Milton Brookins.

The manager of the complex, Jerome Berger, lived in the penthouse of one of the 10 story apartment buildings attached to Laclede Town.

He could stand in his living room and look down upon the utopian little community, as if he were the King of Laclede Town and everyone else was just a serf. In reality, he was the king of Laclede Town. He was appointed by Housing and Urban Development, backed by the federal government, and respected because of Laclede Town's success.

Jerome Berger was a flamboyant character. He owned a vintage Rolls Royce, and he would drive around the property, sometimes with a chauffeur, and gaze at his kingdom.

He desired a racial and cultural balance. He was an intelligent man. He had insight, and he used his insight to place people of races and culture, character and profession, ability, and God given talent, in approximation of one another.

People lived and coexisted with each other, learning and experimenting other cultures and social morays—gleaning intelligence and talent.

Eric Clapton and Mick Jagger once visited just to hang out. They were treated like regulars. No one gawked at or humiliated them.

Radical lawyer William Kunstler came to town to defend some black militants, and played on the Laclede Town

Losers softball team. Joe Pollack, a newsman, founded the Mill Creek Valley Intelligencer newspaper.

World famous tennis champion, Arthur Ashe, who went to high school in St. Louis while in training to be a world champion tennis player, played tennis and gave lessons at the state of the art tennis courts. Tennis became the sport of choice over basketball and football. The partakers of the sport and the lessons from Arthur Ashe were the focal point of the athletic lives in Laclede Town.

After the lessons and matches, the players would meet in the pub at the town square and relive the day's events on the courts. Arthur would calmly advise his students on the strategy and science of the game, and how to take the edge away from their opponents. Arthur was "king of the courts" in Laclede Town.

Laclede Town was part time home to seven year old Eddie Saxon, who became a big-time movie producer, producing "The Silence of The Lambs" and "Philadelphia". Author Warren Fine, who wrote "The Artificial Traveler," lived in Laclede Town.

In its heyday, Laclede Town had 1400 residents. It sat on 65 acres of prime mid-city land. It was the place to be in the City of St. Louis. It was the only government housing project in the country with an outdoor swimming pool.

It stood from 1964 to 1995. Like most of HUD housing projects it was shabbily built. Investors and the government denied money needed to keep the complex in living condition.

The cool and educated hipsters started moving out. Jerome Berger loaded his Rolls Royce and drove out of St. Louis to parts unknown. HUD ripped Laclede Town down to the ground. It sat as a vacant field, weeds and beer cans covered it. St. Louis University again moved to purchase the land. They own it, now.

2

St. Louis Metropolitan Police Patrolman Milton Brookins, his wife and young daughter, lived at 2912 Red Maple Walk, in one of the nifty, new, and clean townhouses in Laclede Town. Milton was born in Mississippi, but he had lived in or around The Mill Creek Valley area of the city as a child.

His family was poor like the other slum dwellers but he had a dad that he knew, and respected, a man who worked at menial jobs to keep food on the table.

Milton was always hungry in his youth, but was never starving the way most of the Mill Creek Valley inhabitants were. There always seemed to be enough money for chicken, and greens, and potatoes, the staple that keeps poor people alive.

He had always been an observer. As an adolescent he walked around the city watching and mentally cataloging the actions of white people. He wondered what made them so different from him.

He would take the Bi-State Bus to University City and walk around in the "Loop" area, watching and listening. On warm days he would walk around the West End of the city where Washington University students lived in high rise apartment buildings---the kind with diagonal stair ways leading upward, left and right with small landings next to each rear door. Most had expensive bicycles chained to the railings.

Milton knew the cost of bicycles. He wanted one but his family couldn't afford such a luxury. The cost of a good bicycle could mean months of chicken and greens for the table.

He had been indoctrinated to hate white people, and he did. As he matured into a man, he realized that he was physically superior to most white men. He was fit, trim and muscular. He jogged and did push-ups, pull ups, and resistance training.

Two of his obsessions were the Civil War, and slavery. He read every book he could get pertaining to slavery. He read about how the wealthy slave owners bred their prize slaves the way ranchers and animal husbandry scientists breed their stock.

During slavery most plantations had "Stud" slaves. These were the biggest, strongest, and most intelligent of all of the male slaves. The owners would then choose the best, brightest and strongest female slave, and would instruct them to breed.

The man, "stud" usually lived in the big house with the white owners families. He was treated better than the other slaves, not required to work in the fields or to do manual labor.

Milton brooded on the stud lifestyle. He figured he was different than the other poor blacks living in the squalor of Mill Creek Valley. He wasn't tall, but his body was muscular cut. He was smarter than his peers, and he had ambition.

Milton figured somewhere in his past, in the huge gene pool that made his being, he was related to a plantation stud.

He was obsessed with white people's vernacular. He longed to listen to them speak to one another. He had learned of the Holocaust in Germany, and had decided that he didn't hate white Jews. They had suffered in much the same manner as American slaves.

When he could he would go to the pawn shops in the city and act like he was shopping. He'd stand in front of the glass cases and gawk at jewelry, guns, and items of intrinsic value. The cost of the items was mind boggling to him, but he wasn't there for the baubles and bangles—he wanted to listen to the Jews banter amongst themselves and with customers.

The Jewish businessmen were always selling, and it appeared that they had the ability to size up their prospective customer shortly after he or she walked through their door. In many cases the customer became the victim. At times Milton would be allowed to stay in the shops and witness the complete transaction between Jewish shop owner and customer.

He learned the beginning, the middle, and the end of a transaction just by watching and listening. Most times the shop owner would roust him, and make him leave the shop. Undaunted he would proceed to another pawn shop. There were several within walking distance.

During his walks he noted the city beat cops. They were on every corner of downtown St. Louis in those days. He would try to stand next to them, to get as close as possible to their massive bodies.

All of them were fat with bellies extending over their cop gun belts. And none of them had a healthy pallor. They reeked of tobacco, and coughed, and many of them reeked of whiskey. He would see them coming and going from the downtown saloons. He'd peer inside through a window, and observe them sitting at the bar, smoking and drinking.

The city cops were physically inferior to him, and to most black men that he knew. But they had guns, and St. Louis cops were noted for using them against black slum dwellers.

When a fat white cop killed a black man in the line of duty, nothing was ever said about it. Even the black slum dwellers accepted the killings.

Milton formed a hypothesis from his observations. The difference between him, a black young man, and the out-of-shape white cops reeking of tobacco, and whiskey, was acceptance. The cops were accepted into St. Louis society because of their jobs, and the fact that they carried pistols. He was not accepted because of his race, even though he was physically superior.

He continued his observations throughout his youth. He liked looking at young white women. They darted in and out of the downtown department stores, and they were always made up just perfectly. They wore tight, revealing clothing and had jewelry shining on their fingers, around their necks, and even on their ankles.

Milton would follow them but knew he could never get away with following them for very long. It was a fleeting obsession with him. He would walk into a department store, and act like he was shopping. The off-duty-cop floor-walker would be standing next to him, shadowing him suspecting he was a shop lifter.

Voyeurism inside the department stores never worked out for him, so he would try to follow them on the street, and make a mental profile on them.

As his life progressed he graduated from high school, got a job in a downtown department store warehouse, and got married. But he was still a slum dweller, still living hand to mouth, and he wasn't accepted into St. Louis society. In the warehouse the white laborers drove fork lifts. The blacks moved heavy boxes by hand.

Milton rationalized his situation. The manual labor made him stronger, and in even better physical shape. In the break room the white people would have conversations with each other. He listened intently.

One of the main topics of conversation was what high school the employees attended. It was a game St. Louis whites used to classify their associates.

In high school Milton lived with his Aunt, Lula Mae Webb, on Vernon Avenue in the west end. He graduated from Soldan High School.

Most of the white people went to parochial schools. If someone answered the question by stating a public school, then that probably meant they weren't Catholic. That fact was looked down upon.

The parochial schools were categorized by how much income the student's parents had. If your parents had big incomes then you would go to an expensive school. There were middle class high schools, and low brow parochial high schools.

Milton was never asked what high school he attended. He was unacceptable on the streets, in the warehouse, and in the break room.

He started carrying a gun. He purchased a 22-caliber pistol from a guy on the street. He bought it for $20.00. It fit nicely in his pants pocket, and it made him feel secure and important.

St. Louis cops, in that era, made a game out of arresting blacks with guns. They would ride around the ghettos in the city and stop cars with black males in them. If the cop didn't self-initiate, the night would drag on and feel as if it would never end.

The cop bosses, who could have been bosses in a sweat shop factory, were pressured to force every cop under their supervision to self-initiate. That meant stopping cars with black occupants, searching them, and their cars and basically humiliating drivers and occupants out of boredom and peer pressure.

The cops would sometimes make bets with each other on which cars had guns in them. They would ride and look at the expressions on the driver's faces. "There's a gun in that car," one would say.

The betting process would begin. "I don't think so," a partner would exclaim.

"Oh yeah? I'll bet you $5.00 there's a gun under the seat."

"You're on!" The cops would activate the red lights and pull the car over. Most of the time the driver had a gun in the car.

It happened to Milton Brookins, his first time actually interacting with St. Louis cops. It was a felony arrest. He was amused by the cops. They handcuffed him and placed him in the back seat of their patrol car. He sat and listened as they laughed and bantered with each other.

It was as if he wasn't in their backseat, listening. He was unsubstantial, as if they had found a lost dog belonging to a rich white woman. They were goofy, playing off of each other like school children as they drove to the station house.

They spoke about their wives, and their children, their love interests, and other cops. They talked too much in front of him, and he observed, and profiled....it was what he did.

After they booked, fingerprinted and photographed him, he felt he knew them. The circuit attorney's office refused the warrant. It was an illegal search and seizure. A felony arrest for the cops, another gun was taken off of the ghetto streets, which was considered "good police work."

Things were looking up for Milton Brookins. On a whim, he took the test to become a St. Louis Metropolitan Police Officer, and he passed it.

He had a lot going for him. He was trim and in shape, physically strong, and he was confident. Appearance is important in law enforcement.

The cop is going into citizens' homes, and interacting with them. Milton was also articulate. He was clean cut, with a full mustache, and a medium afro haircut. He dressed well at the interview, and conducted himself professionally.

The felony gun arrest was overlooked. He advised the high ranking interviewers that he had loaned his car to a friend, and the gun belonged to him. The city needed clean cut, confident, and articulate black police officers. He was hired, and went into the police academy for training.

Shortly after being hired by the St. Louis Metropolitan Police Department, Milton Brookins was accepted as a renter in the utopian Laclede Town housing complex.

Jerome Berger felt that having a clean cut, black, married St. Louis city cop in the neighborhood would give balance and diversity to the populace. Milton and his family fit in and were accepted. Life was good and getting better for him.

The police academy experience is the only time in a cop's life that he or she has normal hours. It's a nine to five gig, sitting in a classroom with thirty other crazy young men and women, most just happy to have a job, some wanting to save the world, some wanting to lead a surreptitious life of crime while carrying a badge, and some with political friends and relatives who would counsel, coddle, and use their influence with the state political system to get them promoted and gain power within the police department.

In reality, while in the academy, you are with your peers and everyone is equal. There are no racial overtones and the world from a police academy candidate perspective is that the world seems ethical and governed by the Constitution of the United States, and the Bill of Rights.

The academy gives the cop the freedom to be himself, but it only lasts sixteen weeks. During that time, Milton enjoyed St. Louis and Laclede Town with his wife and daughter.

In his mind, he had arrived, was accepted into St. Louis society and was his own man. Laclede Town was paradise, whites and blacks were friendly and color seemed not to matter. The residents liked him for what he was, a young, black St. Louis cop with a future.

The academy candidate wears clean clothing, never

misses a meal, exercises regularly, and learns neat and interesting things to talk about at social gatherings. The cop in training leads an ethical, structured life.

After graduating from the academy and going to a district is when the cop realizes that there are no ethics in law enforcement.

He soon is awakened to the fact that race matters in every instance of the job and that if you are a black cop your peers are other black cops, not the white cops you went to the police academy with.

Being confronted with the "real world" aspect of being a big-city cop in a district where you aren't always clean, or freshly worked out, or able to eat good wholesome food at your leisure, or well rested with at least eight hours of sleep a night changes the demeanor of some cops.

Add to that the glaring racial divide of a city like St. Louis, Missouri, and you have the recipe for an unhappy cop, carrying a gun, a badge, and a bad attitude. Some cops get over it and realize the cop job is just a job, nothing more, nothing less.

Milton could not rationalize himself through the maze of problems associated with being a black man and a district cop. He subsequently reacted against the "white devil" in the manner he had been taught as a child.

3

Probationary Patrolman Milton Brookins graduated from the St. Louis Metropolitan Police Academy in September of 1965. He was assigned to the Carondelet District, AKA the First Police District.

On the surface there seemed nothing unusual about this assignment. The first district was a neat place, the first outpost (1767) in the Midwest not controlled by the French. Everything on the east side of the river was French controlled. The west side was controlled by the Spanish.

Clement Delor de Tregret settled in the area. It was approximately five miles south of a small outpost named St. Louis.

Delor spotted a small valley that opened onto the west bank of the Mississippi River. A limestone bluff on the north, a ridge on the west, and a set of hills on the south framed the valley.

Delor built a stone house near the Mississippi River for himself, his wife and his two daughters. He built a small town there, and it became occupied by Creoles (people of Spanish and French descent) who built houses, a church and a cemetery.

In 1794 Delor named the outpost Carondelet in honor of the Baron Francois Louis Hector de Carondelet. Needless to say, the Carondelet District had history and character. The ornate police "station house" sat across from Carondelet Park, one of the stately neighborhood parks in the southern part of the city.

South St. Louis is geographically determined by Chouteau Avenue, which runs from the Mississippi River, west to the county line.

The imaginary line was drawn in the sand by city fathers in the early 19th century. Blacks were supposed to stay north of Chouteau Avenue. Being a Southsider in the City of St. Louis had meaning. It means "I'm white and I don't want to live with any Negroes".

Probationary Patrolman Milton Brookins was the first black cop ever assigned to the Carondelet Police District. The city, the Police Board, and the newspapers made a big deal about Milton's assignment. Somewhere in some dark and dank office in police headquarters, a high ranking cop thought this would be a good idea.

It may have been a good idea for the police department, but it was not a good or fair idea for Milton Brookins. He was not welcomed with open arms.

The cops in the Carondelet District, young and old, took pride in their whiteness, and the whiteness of the district populace. There was a small section (maybe two blocks) behind the station house where some blacks lived, but 99.9 % of the populace was white. No public housing or high rises.

But most of the residents were poor, living hand to mouth just like the poor blacks in north St. Louis. The difference between poor city blacks and poor city whites is subsistence, and employment. Whites could get jobs, and their assistance from state and federal governments was limited.

But both races had the same cultural problems---booze, drugs, poor choices, and poor attitudes. Speaking to a poor white Carondelet citizen was just like talking to a poor black north side resident. If you closed your eyes you couldn't tell the difference.

As in all neighborhoods there was a ritzy area with brick designed homes. Holly Hills was designed to replicate Hollywood, California neighborhoods in the 1920's. Lawyers, doctors, politicians, and some high ranking cops lived there.

Phantom Rapist

There were neighborhoods where the streets were named after states. There were areas down by the Mississippi River that were close to being slums (not as bad as Mill Creek Valley) but still slummy. The district was the third largest of the nine districts within the City of St. Louis.

Milton hit the ground running the way all new cops do. It is as hectic as any profession, until you get the hang of the job. That usually takes about three years. Probationary cops, back in the day, were only on probation two months after graduation from the police academy. After two months Milton was "on his own".

The white populace of the southern-most district prided themselves on calling the cops at any given moment, and when they called, the police dispatcher sent a patrol car to their house or business without hesitation.

On the day watch most of what the district cops did was to smooth talk the callers, use police community relations tactics, and slide back into their patrol cars for a quick free lunch.

It doesn't take long to figure out what survival in a cop car is all about. The name of the game is, "tell them what they want to hear". In about a year Milton, and hundreds like him, quickly come to the realization that justice is fleeting, if not imaginary, and that most victims set themselves up to become victims.

He realized that street criminals seldom get captured shortly after their crime. The ones who were captured, and were black were taken to the detective bureau, and beaten. Cops got in their faces and screamed at them: "Keep your black ass north of Chouteau, boy!"

The cops seemed to always be in the wrong place at the wrong time, and the criminals always seemed to have a plan to elude instant capture. Most of them get caught later on, after investigation, or after they brag about their crime and are informed upon.

In his observations he realized that white victims cannot properly identify black people. Maybe because of fear, or the initial shock of becoming a victim; or just because all black people look the same to white people. He figured that blacks were put on this earth as the perfect criminal, strong, quick, determined, relentless, and brutal, and to reinforce his theory---- unidentifiable.

After three or four years the seasoned cop realizes that if there wasn't booze, drugs, or hookers, there wouldn't be any real need for cops---maybe just a few in each of the districts.

Milton rode alone most of the time. He occasionally had a white partner, and he would converse with the white cops. It was the same old rock and roll; "What did you do before becoming a cop? What are your long range plans?"

It was boring, and Milton felt slighted. The white cops would drink after duty on the afternoon watch. They'd all meet up on a vacant lot somewhere in the district and have sex and beer parties.

There was a van with several fat and homely country girls (referred to as Munchkins) who would ride around the southern districts giving cold beer, food, and oral sex to the young and foolish cops.

If a cop was parked for any amount of time, the van would pull up, and provide the cops with beer, food, and an invitation to a lot party after he got off of work. The Munchkins trolled the southern districts. They never went north of Chouteau.

One of the girls was in the United States Air Force, stationed at Scott Air Base on the eastside. The crazy young white cops liked her, and nicknamed her "Air Force One".

On a steamy summer night on the afternoon watch an overzealous young cop keyed his microphone and stated, "Air Force One has landed." This was code that their favorite party girl would be in attendance at the lot party after the shift ended. Air Force One would service dozens of young cops in an evening. One of the young south side cops overlooked her seamy past, and married her.

Milton was never invited to the lot parties. He asked a white riding partner about it and was advised that blacks were not invited. He felt slighted, but he rationalized that the women were fat and unattractive. He desired more from a sex partner.

And to add insult to injury, his supervisor, acting Sergeant Harry Freeman, demanded that he write traffic violation tickets. He hated writing the tickets. He'd set up on a stop sign and wait for some white hillbilly to violate the sign.

He tried to be polite, calling the country bumpkins "sir" and "ma'am" but it never failed. After he got them to sign the ticket and while he was walking away they'd call him a "niggar".

It takes confidence to not overreact. Milton had confidence, and he was satisfied with his life. He loved going to the Laclede Town pool, and ogling the white girls in their bikinis.

He had this thing for young white women, and he didn't know why. They flirted with him on calls. And at times he would flirt back. He attributed it to his being in shape, looking good in his uniform, and just for being a St. Louis cop. But he always attributed it to being a descendant of a slave stud.

He could also talk, thanks to the Jewish pawn shop owners, and sell himself to the country, young, white girls on the streets. Many "hung out" in front of their parents houses just to flag down, and talk to a St. Louis cop. Milton was amazed that they spoke like residents of Mill Creek Valley.

He was amazed that ambitious black folks strived to speak like white folks. It helped them to progress in the job market, and in white society. But these white girls strived to speak like black people.

It was a situation wherein the whites didn't need to be ambitious---they were already white, and they were deemed superior to any black, ambitious, educated or even rich. But they didn't feel superior to any St. Louis cop. Most of the Carondelet cops were respected and admired. They were silent heroes riding the neighborhoods in their cop cars. The ones who would be there when they were needed----would stop when flagged down, and who would not tread upon any soul unless it was necessary.

To most of these uneducated, poor and struggling white country girls straight from the "Boot Heel" the color of the cop did not matter. If he looked good, and was a St. Louis cop, then that was enough for a sexual interlude.

There were several young white girls that he would stop, and talk to during his shift. Cops have down time, especially in the southern most district of the city. The two or three girls he made friends with eventually became sex partners with him.

He wouldn't go home right after work, and he would tell his wife that he had to work overtime. Cops in those days didn't get paid overtime, so his wife couldn't check up on him by perusing his pay stub.

His infatuation with white women became an obsession. He rented an apartment with a twenty year old white south-sider, and they split the rent. He only spent a couple of hours a day there but he felt it was worth it.

He had another white girlfriend in the district, and he would meet her in Carondelet Park after dark. They would have sex in the police car. Some days he would have sex with both of them during the same shift. He gave each of them an engagement ring.

Acting Sergeant Harry Freeman knew Milton's girlfriends. They were always standing in front of their wood clapboard houses waving at the district cops. If a cop stopped they would proudly display the engagement ring gift from Patrolman Milton Brookins, and brag about their romance with the handsome young copper.

Acting Sergeant Harry Freeman had been in the Carondelet District most of his life. He knew almost all of the businessmen, and most of the residents. They all knew him, and they would praise or complain about the district cops to him. Harry was the "go to" guy for the poor folk of Carondelet. Harry spotted Milton as a troubled individual, and took an interest in him.

Milton's demeanor changed. He grew from confident to cocky. His gait changed, and he grew obnoxious to be around. He stopped having sex with his wife. He only wanted white women.

His neighbors at Laclede Town noted a difference in him. He constantly washed his car, and he was obsessed with cleanliness.

Someone stole Acting Sergeant Harry Freeman's raincoat from the district supervisor's office. Harry was always an acting supervisor. The police department was controlled by the State of Missouri, a law enacted during the Civil War to keep the police department from being used as a militia against the Union Army.

And there were the ever present St. Louisans who had clout within the state legislature and urged their children to go into the police department. Their cronyism with state politicians was a sure fire way to be promoted to sergeant, and obtain an office job in headquarters.

The cops with outside power flaunted their royalty. They were the "chosen ones" in the St. Louis cop scene. In the "poor boy" cop game, they were considered "born rich". To the casual observer the whole promotional process was a joke.

The political appointees would do a short stint in the southern district, and then leave for greener pastures in the downtown headquarters building, commonly referred to as the "Ivory tower".

There was always a shortage of supervisors in the Carondelet District, so the cop with the most seniority was made an acting sergeant.

Cops lose their equipment all of the time. They leave their raincoats in the police cars and when the oncoming shift comes on, the cop steals it.

Some cops are pilferers. They feel they are entitled to anything that catches their eye. Stealing a police department raincoat is mild for the pilfering cops.

Acting Sergeant Freeman, in confidence, mentioned to one of his crew that he felt Patrolman Milton Brookins stole his police department raincoat. That's all it took for a character assassination squad of cops to start the rumor that Milton was a thief. He overheard a couple of cops stating, "That niggar cop in the eleven area stole the sarge's raincoat."

Milton endured. He wasn't about to give up his cop job, his groovy townhouse, his car and his white girlfriends because of a rumor. The cop who spread the rumor was probably the one who stole the sarge's raincoat.

Harry Freeman was an honest old time city cop. He was embarrassed, and humiliated by the antics of the younger cops. He kept a mental tab on all of the Carondelet District cops. It's what cops do; we catalog events. It becomes a natural occurrence in our lives.

Harry befriended Milton Brookins. He acted as a mentor to Milton. There are no secrets among cops in a police precinct. Everybody knows everyone else's business. Harry knew Milton had a "thing" for young white girls. But it was not an unusual occurrence within the confines of the police culture. In fact it was a mild indulgence considering the thievery, drinking, and whore mongering occurring within the ranks of the cops.

Harry would preach to Milton. An old cop can spot a troubled individual from a block away. Milton confided in Harry. Harry listened, and didn't inform the watch commander or district commander of Milton's indiscretions.

Harry figured Milton was on the path to ruination. He just didn't know what method Milton would use to completely self-destruct.

When we go home at the end of a shift we vent to our wives. Our children are listening to our conversations. They draw conclusions. Milton Brookins was a mainstay of information for the Freeman family. The only black cop in a white/racist community was better entertainment than late 60's television.

Milton would go out at night sometimes with his uniform on. He'd tell his wife that he had work to do, and he'd drive to the West End, and walk around the neighborhood, looking into windows. He was obsessed with the West End of the city, named for its western boundary with St. Louis County, because it had young white female students living in apartments.

There were students from Washington University living there. There were medical and nursing students from Jewish Hospital, and there were the expensive bicycles on the crisscrossed stairways leading upward from apartment to apartment with windows on every walkway.

On one summer night, while in uniform, he came across a city cop walking toward an apartment, going on a call. Milton was startled that the cop observed him. He asked

Milton why he was in his area with his uniform on.

Milton didn't have a feasible answer. The cop advised his supervisor that an off-duty Carondelet District cop was walking around on his beat in uniform. Milton was disciplined for the indiscretion. There was an order against cops wearing their uniform off-duty.

Milton continued his late night walks around the Washington University apartments. He kept getting closer to climbing onto the stairwells and actually looking into the landing windows.

On a crisp fall night he went to an apartment house that didn't have a gate securing the ground level stairway. He had access to approximately 20 windows to peer into. He started on the second floor and made his way up. He fixated on a comely nursing student doing her homework at the kitchen table.

He stared at her, longing to tap on the window and have her come to him, unlock the window and invite him inside. He heard a district scout car approaching his location. The cop had the window down and the loud police radio alerted Milton.

Milton, according to a witness in another building, couldn't take the stairway down or he would have met up with the cop parking his car. He climbed and shimmied down from each level, on the side of the apartment house like a monkey where the cop couldn't observe him. He escaped.

The witness, who was actually the caller, informed the cops about the antics of the peeping Tom. It was an athletic event that few men could perform.

The next day at roll call in the seventh district the patrolmen were advised to watch out for a peeping Tom. They nick named him the "monkey burglar" and gave a description of a Negro male in his twenties wearing dark clothing.

The nine police districts were connected by teletype machines. The only computer was in headquarters. Most cops in those ancient days had never heard of a computer.

If something interesting or suspicious came across the teletype machine from another district it was read at roll calls at all of the districts. The teletype concerning the "monkey burglar" was read at all roll calls. Milton had to have heard the roll call alert.

The cops in the Carondelet district laughed about the depiction of the "monkey burglar". They didn't know it but they were laughing at the cop standing with them at roll call.

Milton was not deterred. A couple of nights later Milton was back in the West End peering into windows. There was a police detail on foot in the vicinity trying to catch him.

Milton was on the second floor of a stairway landing watching a young nurse. The victim went to the door and opened it. A seventh district cop entered the apartment, and ran toward the landing door where Milton was crouched.

Milton knew what had transpired---that he had been observed, and that there was probably another cop on the ground level waiting for him.

He leapt from the second floor stairway landing onto the ground, rolled one time, jumped up, and ran away. Both cops, the one on the landing, and the one on the ground observed him flying through the air.

The cop on the ground chased Milton on foot but couldn't get anywhere near him. Milton was too fast, too nimble, the perfect criminal, and the cops couldn't give a description of him; just a Negro male, approximately 5'10, weighing 160 pounds.

Milton's physical ability, and his determination to elude capture unnerved the cops. They referred to him as the "Phantom". The "monkey burglar" depiction was forgotten.

Milton now had a new moniker. The press would eventually eat it up.

Milton came to work the next day with a limp. He was the Phantom, not the "monkey burglar". It was time to change his tactics. A phantom needed to drive a car that befit him.

His wife, Cecelia drove him to a downtown Avis rental car business looking for a phantom type of a vehicle. She didn't know why he desired such a vehicle but she was at the point of no return in their marriage. She had nowhere to go. Poor folks are trapped in their relationships.

He observed a dark blue, almost black 1969 Chevrolet two door sitting on the lot. It had a black vinyl top, and Milton was mesmerized by it. He parked, and examined the vehicle. It had tan interior, and a V-8 engine, and something new at the time, an F.M. stereo radio.

Milton had pilfered a Shell credit card during an exploratory mission on the Campus of Washington University. He would go there and walk around, like a student. He was testing the waters of the staff at the university. He wanted to know if he would ever be challenged, or questioned as to why he was there. He looked like a foreign student, maybe from Africa, or the islands.

He would sometimes wander into the offices of teachers, and professors. People in the offices would smile at him, and offer him coffee. He became brazen, and entered a professor's office. He asked to talk with the professor, knowing he was not in his office but in class, stating he was supposed to wait for the professor until he showed up after a class.

The secretary invited him to sit in one of the comfortable office chairs and wait for the professor. She left Milton alone in the office while she went to the restroom.

Milton went into the professor's private office, and rifled his desk. The professor's wallet was in the desk. Milton removed a credit card from the back of the wallet. It looked like it hadn't been used. He pocketed it, and left the office.

The name on the Shell credit card was Michael Constant. Milton took out his trusty traffic ticket book, and wrote out a red light traffic violation for Michael Constant. When citizens get a traffic ticket they can either volunteer their driver's license to the cop for bail, or get booked and make bail at the station house. The copy of the traffic summons is used as their driver's license.

He entered the car rental office and told the clerk he wanted to rent the dark blue Chevrolet. He was given a rental agreement form, and he filled it out, placing Professor Michael Constant's name, erroneous address and telephone number on the form. He told the clerk he would return the rental in two days.

He handed the form back to the clerk, and as the clerk was examining it Milton showed him his stolen Shell credit card and the copy of the red violation traffic summons.

"Oh, yes sir," the clerk replied. The deal was sealed. Milton drove off in the phantom rental. Milton had long range plans for the rest of his life. His wife, Cecilia, his closest ally in the game of survival in the "white devil's" society knew nothing of Milton's desire for young white women.

Milton dropped Cecelia off at their townhome and cruised the streets of the Central West End and the West End. Young white women walked without fear, rode bicycles late at night and were oblivious to the dangers of the street.

But Milton didn't wish to assault and rape anyone who was a pedestrian or bike rider. He desired young white women who were inside their residences.

People feel safe and content in their domiciles. If they answer their door and are pistol paralyzed by the person in the doorway, they will do whatever they are told to do. And there is always a bed or couch for Milton to order them to.

His plan was coming together.

4

Milton decided to concentrate his efforts in the entire West End of the city. His plans included the Central West End which bounded Kingshighway on the west, Boyle on the east, Lindell on the south, and Olive on the north.

The "West End" went all the way to the county line. He stayed away from St. Louis County. Blacks stand out there, he would be noticed.

He drove the area during daylight when he was off duty. Pershing was a street of interest. The brick multi-storied apartment houses were jam packed into each other on Pershing, separated by gangways, and there was an alley on both sides of Pershing.

There wasn't any off street parking, and the street was always crowded with cars parked at the curb. Students from Washington University occupied these apartments, although there were some professional people living in condominiums scattered among the apartment buildings.

The film "The Boston Strangler" had just come out. He took Cecelia to see it. He imagined himself as a black Tony Curtis. The movie gave him insight on how to enter victim's residences. He was no longer going to be a nighttime phantom.

Victims tend to answer their doors during the daylight hours. He had knocked on thousands of doors in the past four years as a cop. During the day watch the Carondelet District inhabitants always opened their doors without saying "who's there?"

All Milton needed was an open door, and he would take charge of the situation. He knew what to do. Whites are terrified of black people. Place a gun to the head of any white person and they will comply with any command. He was the Phantom, and he struck fear in the hearts of white women.

When Mill Creek Valley was condemned his dad left the family looking for work. The last words his dad had for him were, "Go out and populate the world."

Milton's mother went into the Pruitt Igoe Housing Projects. She didn't want Milton to grow up as a teenager in the projects. She took him to her sister, Lula Mae Webb. Lula Mae had a house at 5133 Vernon Avenue, just a block or so west of Kingshighway, just a short distance from Washington University.

Many of the female Washington University students came from liberal families. Washington University was known for its liberal ideology.

Milton heard some of the older West End kids talking about going to apartments on Pershing and sexually servicing the rich white girls. The talk on the street was that the rich girls from Washington University wanted to experience sex with black men. Sometimes they would pay for their experience.

Lula Mae Webb opened her home to Milton. She knew he had a problem. Milton's mother advised Lula Mae that Milton had a mental problem but if she just took him until he finished his last four years and graduated from high school he might turn out all right. It was an experiment.

Lula Mae told her neighbors and friends that Milton was a "sick little boy", and pointed to her head whenever she got the chance. Milton had to have heard her description of him, and seen her antics.

Milton befriended a boy five years younger than him. He didn't live on Vernon but he was a West End kid. His name was William Robinson, a mulatto child, and like Milton he too was a loner.

Milton would take William with him for walks around

Washington University. They talked incessantly. William knew Milton better than any other human. He wanted to fashion his life after Milton. In fact, William became a St. Louis cop, was in the police academy with the author of this true-crime book. We were both assigned to the bloody ninth district and rode together for years.

Patrolman William Robinson spoke of Milton Brookins to me during the cold, long night shifts of misery in the bloody ninth district. He visited Milton while he was incarcerated in the City Jail. He took him food and toiletries.

Milton had done his dastardly deeds to the white women of the West End, and the Central West End, and was rotting in the Missouri State Penitentiary during our conversations.

Patrolman Robinson didn't defend Milton Brookins, but he explained him to me. Milton was indeed a sick little boy. Milton was, and is ancient history, just as the ways of law enforcement and investigation were ancient, the rights and protections of victims were also ancient. Especially rape victims.

Rape victims were not taken seriously by the police, the prosecutors, the judges, or the juries. There was no sex crime unit or rape squad to investigate alleged rapes. Most times rape victims were not offered medical treatment. If they needed treatment they were on their own, and had to convey themselves to the emergency room.

There was hardly ever any collection of evidence at the crime scene, and there was no evidence technician called to process a rape scene, unless it was a homicide.

The patrolman investigating at the scene made the determination whether fingerprints should be taken from the scene. In the report, which was hand written, the scene cop would write, "prints not taken due to contamination at scene".

The rule of thumb at rape scenes was to get the victims

statement, get a description of the alleged rapist, collect the panties of the victim, and leave the scene.

The collection of panties was a big deal, and if the investigating cop forgot the panties he was instructed to return to the scene and seize them. Most times the victim would refuse to open the door for the cop. Or she would hand the panties to him from an ajar door with a chain on it, or through a transom above the door.

The "panties as evidence" collection came from an alleged rape case from years earlier. A cop was on the stand testifying in a rape case. The prosecutor, the judge, and the jury were smug and disbelieving, and the defense attorney was intent on getting his client off.

He tried to instill in the jury that the sex between his client and the victim was consensual, and that they were in fact lovers, and had been for a lengthy amount of time.

The defense attorney asked the testifying cop if he seized any evidence at the crime scene. The cop replied, "No sir."

The cop had testified earlier that the victim advised him that the perpetrator had removed the panties from the victim's body. "You didn't seize the panties?" the defense attorney asked.

"No sir," the cop replied.

"Why not?" the defense asked.

"Because they weren't on her body when your client had sex with her," he replied. "They had been removed."

The defense attorney had an opening, and he made the best of it. He talked about evidence, and the fact that his client did not tear the panties, and that they were gently removed by the victim because she desired sex with his client. The rapist was acquitted.

State prosecutors do not like to lose cases. They usually take cases that they can win. Most cases are refused at the prosecutor's office. They thought they could win this one.

They were wrong, and upset by the acquittal.

A memorandum from the Circuit Attorney's office was mailed to the Chief's office. "Please instruct your personnel to seize panties of alleged rape victims, and to package them as evidence."

It made life easier for the patrolman. Report to an alleged rape scene, get vital information, seize panties, leave scene. Job done! The bosses were happy, the Circuit Attorney's office was satisfied, and the victim, who was never queried, and whose violated body, and mind did not matter, was non-important. Only the cops, the prosecutors, and the judges knew the big secret in the criminal justice system: there is no justice.

Milton prowled the Pershing and Washington University area. His interest in expensive bicycles, something he could never have, aided him in his mission. He knew the makes and prices of good bikes. His knowledge of bicycles helped him in his quest to pursue and victimize white women.

In Mill Creek Valley, and in the West End neighborhood of Lula Mae Webb, the neighborhoods of his late teens, one of the utterances of ignorance was, "if the "white devil" denies you something, then you must take it from him or her. It is rightfully yours".

White women had not denied him sex. The hillbilly white women in the Carondelet District accepted him, sexually, but he desired sex from a different kind of white woman---educated, rich, beautiful, and cultured. If he was denied, he would take what he desired.

He studied the bicycles chained to the crisscrossed stairways at the back of the apartments at 5349 Pershing Avenue. He saw a Columbia man's bike with the seat down all the way. No man would ride with the seat down. It had to belong to a white woman student.

Her apartment was on the third floor near the northwest

quadrant of the apartment building. There was no apartment either north or west of her apartment, just a hallway and apartments lining it to the south and east.

He purchased some books, and a note pad and drove down Skinker Boulevard towards Washington University, parked his dark blue Phantom rental on a side street near the campus, then walked to the campus and mingled with the students.

He looked the part. He could have been a graduate student, or even maybe an instructor. The students were friendly to him, nodding and speaking to him in friendly tones as they scurried to class in the cold and gloom of St. Louis winter. There were no disparaging remarks, no insults or looks of wonder.

He worked his way to the bike racks at the west end of the campus. He studied the bicycles; he recognized many of them. He observed the Colombia Bicycle from the apartment on Pershing. He waited to see who would eventually claim it, and ride away on it toward Pershing.

He continued to walk to and fro, mingling with the offspring of the elite of the world, constantly monitoring the bike stand. It was his first day off in an eight day stretch, and he had nothing better to do.

One of the reasons St. Louis cops remain in their profession is because of the days off. Cops are given a schedule for the year showing when the shift changes, and when their days off are. They are accumulated in bunches. A cop might work ten day stretches, then have three days off, then six or seven day stretches, and have eight days off. And to top it off there is a twenty one day vacation period every year. Returning to work after the long off-day stretches is difficult.

A comely brunette was walking toward the bike rack. She unlocked the Colombia bicycle, placed her book bag on the rack on the back, and peddled toward Pershing. She was about perfect for Milton----young, vivacious and fit.

Milton figured she was probably from the east coast, and that her parents were probably paying about $30,000 a year for her to attend college in St. Louis----more than his parents made in five years, excluding food stamps and welfare.

It was noon on January 29th, 1969. Milton slowly walked toward the dark blue Phantom rental parked on the side street. He wasn't anxious. He'd know if his potential victim was in her apartment. He just had to drive down the alley, and look for the Colombia ten speed on the porch landing.

He gave her approximately thirty minutes, then he slowly drove down the alley. The Colombia was there. He drove north and parked on Delmar, three blocks from the apartment building on Pershing. He slowly walked south in the cold, and wind approaching the Pershing address from the east.

He had his confident gait as he bounded up the concrete stairway and into the unlocked door of the apartment building. He took the stairway up to the third floor not encountering anyone. There was very little noise---no radio or television sound, and no one talking.

He came to her apartment door, paused, then knocked lightly three times. She came to the door immediately, opened it and was confronted by Milton Brookins holding a silver pistol to her face. The sight of him, and the pistol paralyzed her with fear. He knew it would. He pushed the door open and grabbed her by the blouse as he pushed the door shut with his foot. "Don't scream or talk or I'll kill you," he calmly said to her. She stood and stared at him.

Milton took a quick look around the apartment. It was a one bedroom. "If you cooperate with me I won't hurt you," he began. "Take off all of your clothing."

She complied.

"Go into the bedroom and get on the bed."

She complied.

He stuck the silver revolver in his pants pocket then removed all of his clothing. He mounted her on the bed, and had intercourse with her for approximately twenty minutes--- finished the sex act, backed off and stared at her.

He dressed, and then questioned her as to where she kept her cash hidden in the apartment. She told him there was some cash in a kitchen drawer in an envelope. He went to the kitchen and took the cash; it was approximately $50.00.

He ordered her to go into the bathroom and not to come out. She complied, and after a few minutes she thought she heard him leave the apartment. She came out, dressed, and telephoned her husband. Her husband advised her to call the police.

Milton calmly walked north toward Delmar to the Phantom Rental. He walked past a seventh district cop car at the intersection. One of the cops was talking on the call box-- the other cop was sitting in the car. Milton read their name tags. He looked them right in the eyes as he strolled by them.

He listened for sirens as he walked, but he knew that when the victim called the police they would take their sweet time getting to the crime scene.

He drove the Phantom Rental back to the scene on Pershing and parked. The cops weren't there yet. Maybe she hadn't called them. Milton wanted the cops called. The rape act was only part of the thrill he needed to survive.

He wanted to watch the inept city cops stumbling, and bungling over each other at the crime scene. He wished he could have been hiding in the apartment while they interviewed the victim. He wanted to observe their disbelief. He wanted to see their faces as they shot glances at each other.

In most rape cases the radio dispatchers were instructed not to place a rape call out over the radio. Instead the cop was instructed to go to a call box (most of them were inoperable) and then the cop would get the assignment to go to the rape scene.

If the rape assignment was given out over the air there would be cops from all over the city responding there to gawk at the victim, mill around the scene, and possibly contaminate evidence from the house or apartment.

Finally a cop car was slowly driving down the street. Milton parked a half block away and watched through the rear view mirror of the Phantom Rental. Milton watched as the cop exited his police vehicle, and walked into the building.

Patrolman John Keplinger in charge of radio car Ocean seven had gotten the call to the rape scene. When cops go into a crime scene their senses are on high. Instinctively they examine every square inch of the scene, and then focus their attention on the victim. They subconsciously dissect the victim. They decipher every nuance muttered by them, every body movement or action the victim emits is analyzed by the first responder cop.

John's instincts assured him that this was indeed a true crime, and not a boyfriend girlfriend escapade. During his initial interview of the twenty two year old victim he learned that she was a person of faith, and that her husband was also.

Milton continued to watch. In approximately ten more minutes, an unmarked vehicle came onto the scene and entered the building. It was the watch commander and the precinct sergeant. They were inside for approximately thirty minutes and then the supervisors left.

The paddy wagon showed up at the scene. It was the

conveyance to City Hospital # one, the white man's hospital. If a victim wished to go to another hospital then he/she had to make those arrangements on their own. Except if the victim was black, then he/she would be taken to Homer G. Phillips Hospital.

Patrolman Keplinger seized the victim's panties, and the bed sheets, packaged them, and instructed the cruiser driver to convey the victim to City Hospital # one. Milton continued to watch while they drove right past him as he sat in the Phantom Rental.

Milton was well aware that in most rape cases the cops were disbelieving. The victim was always in the wrong. They would mentally classify the incident as that of a black boy-friend getting wild with his white girlfriend. Milton drove home, satisfied, content, and already planning his next conquest.

Milton was a satisfied man, sexually and mentally. He had punished the "white devil" in the manner he was taught. It was a successful crime committed by him against the enemy, and it was non-violent.

Milton was prepared to become violent if needed. Violence was not needed in this rape and robbery. He hoped that somewhere down the road in his quest for rape victims violence would be called for.

5

The seventh police district in the City of St. Louis was known to be the wildest of the nine districts. It was commonly referred to as the "Wild West".

Each police district is like a small town police department. The population of the seventh was approximately 30,000 citizens, and 85% of that population was black.

As in most of the city police districts there was an area consisting of wealthy residents. Around Lindell Boulevard and to the north there were private streets with ornate granite mansions on them.

The mansions are cherished like rare works of art. The residents hire off-duty cops and private security companies to patrol around their private streets.

The apartment houses around Washington University were owned by old money real estate investors who lived in the mansions on the private streets, or wealthier families living in West St. Louis County.

The wealthy folks didn't care of the plight of the poor; their concern was keeping the poor blacks and their social problems out of their neighborhoods. That is where the seventh police district personnel came into play.

Each police district had a detective bureau attached to it, run solely at the discretion of the commander of the district. He determined who would be a detective, and who would be the detective sergeant.

In most of the police districts the downtown bureaucrats in cubbyhole offices in police headquarters would pressure the district captain to place their friends and relatives in district detective bureaus. That wasn't exactly the case in the "Wild West" seventh police district.

One of the perks of being in the seventh was the fact that nobody in headquarters gave a damn what happened out there. It was far enough away, and predominantly black. Most of the bureaucrats had never been to the district. They did their street time in places like the Carondelet district where everybody looked like them, spoke like them, and shared insight with them.

The seventh police district was like a foreign land. The station house was situated on a square city block at Union and Page. It looked like a haunted house. It was three stories, made of wood clapboard and had a giant cupola.

In reality it wasn't a haunted house, it was a torture chamber for errant blacks. Getting snagged by a seventh district cop equated to a sure fire beating while being handcuffed to a steel chair. It was acceptable behavior by everyone involved: the courts, the cops, even the blacks being beaten.

The downtown cop bureaucrats wouldn't even drive their department staff cars on streets out in the seventh for fear of becoming involved in an altercation, one they were not prepared to deal with.

The Captain, or Commander of the seventh was Barney Mundt. He was a schmoozer who smoked big cigars and wore nice suits. He was a politician who felt he had earned his commander status through great police work (they all do) but in reality there is always a politician hiding in the family tree, guiding the political cop through the maze of political promotions.

But by being in the "Wild West" seventh Barney had leverage to move young cops in and out of the detective bureau. If you went to a district detective bureau then you have "arrived" in the game of law enforcement in the City of St. Louis, Missouri.

The next step would be to go to a bureau in headquarters,

and drive a personal staff car, or maybe get promoted to sergeant and be a leader of a squad of young cops, or maybe get hired by a federal law enforcement agency, and get transferred to Arizona, California, or Florida.

The detective sergeant of the district bureaus was usually appointed by the chief of police, except in the seventh. It wasn't a job intelligent or politically connected people wished for. At that time the chief was Curtis Brostron. He was nearing the mandatory retirement age, and political bureaucrats were jockeying for leverage to take his place.

As in any small town (Wild West seventh) the town chief, or sheriff, usually has a fairly good idea who the culprits of crime are. The detective sergeant is compelled to, and has the responsibility to clean up or clear crimes in his district. It is his responsibility.

In many criminal cases a crime is cleared by an arrest. It isn't precisely mandatory that the correct person is arrested----just that the crime is cleared. The circuit attorney's office hardly ever issues warrants on questionable cases, so the real culprit remains free, the arrested subject is released due to lack of evidence, and the crime is cleared.

This practice is referred to as "good police work" and cops are praised, and awarded for clearing crimes. The practice makes the detective sergeant, the detectives, and the district captain look like great cops.

This rape of the student on Pershing was haunting Detective Sergeant Chester Blancett, the commander, Captain Barney Mundt, and most of the caring detectives in the seventh district detective bureau.

Detective Sergeant Blancett assigned the rape case on Pershing to his two most caring detectives: Detective George Hotsenpiller, and Detective Bobby Matthews.

Both detectives were country boys. Bobby Matthews grew up on the Missouri State Penitentiary work farm; his dad was the warden for the penitentiary.

George Hotsenpiller hailed from Monroe County, Missouri, and was raised on a cattle, hog and grain farm. The closest town to his dad's farm was Florence, Missouri. It was a Saturday night town; farmers went to town on Saturday nights, got drunk, got into fights with other farmers, and then went to church on Sunday morning.

George's dad died at the age of fifty four. George's mom had to sell the farm, and George joined the United States Marine Corps at the tender age of seventeen.

After three years in the Corps, George moved to the big-city of St. Louis. He worked in construction, belonged to a couple of trade unions, and then applied for the cop job. Having been in the Marine Corps is a positive step toward being a St. Louis cop.

George liked the cop work. He was assigned to the downtown district, and after a year in uniform he was transferred to the 4th district detective bureau. He liked being a district detective, but he was offered a job in a specialized unit in the Bureau of Investigation.

Prestige intrigued him, and he accepted the job. But he wasn't there for long. When a cop is in a specialized unit other cops desire his job. He was "aced out" and got transferred to the "Wild West" seventh district, a place you are thrust into and forgotten about.

But George still worked hard. He stopped cars, got guns off of the street, locked up the "bad guys" and became noticed again by his superiors. He was asked if he wanted to go to the seventh district detective bureau, and he accepted.

He teamed up with Bobby Matthews, and they both enjoyed each other, and their jobs. There's always someone to investigate or lock up in the "Wild West" seventh. It was a fun way to make a living.

The day after the rape of Milton Brookins first victim at

5349 Pershing, Detectives Hotsenpiller and Matthews went to her apartment to interview her. They had photos of area rapists, and they were seeking more information on the black guy who was raping white women.

She was shown the photos; she could not make any identification. George was making an attempt to be kind to the victim. Bobby Matthews, who was usually intoxicated or hung over said, "Was the guy hung?"

The victim looked blankly at him. "You know what I'm saying? Did he have a big dong? Was he big?" Bobby was using his hands as a measuring device.

"Is there a female detective I can talk with," she calmly asked.

"Well," George interrupted, "That's all for now," he muttered, "We'll be in touch if we get any information on this perpetrator, Thank You, ma'am." He ushered Bobby toward the door and they left.

There were two other cops interested in the rape. They were uniform cops, and their area was the 5300 block of Pershing: Patrolman Ron Adler and Sam Lackland. They were waiting for Detectives Hotsenpiller and Matthews to return to their detective car so they could pick their brains.

Most uniform guys are waiting in line to become detectives. Ron Adler and Sam Lackland wanted information that could possibly help them identify a guy on the street, stop him and bring him into the detective bureau.

"Any new information on the rape?" Ron Adler asked.

"Nope," George replied. "Same as yesterday, black guy 5'10, medium complexion, mid- twenties."

"With a big dick," Bobby Matthews shouted to them as he climbed into the detective car. George climbed in, started the engine and they sped off. Ron and Sam Lackland continued their patrols around the Pershing area.

Ron Adler was a handsome man. He was tall, well-proportioned with good features and a full head of hair. He had striking blue eyes, and had the nickname of "Frosty O's" because of his round and blue eyes.

    He was a conscientious cop, and he really cared about his victims. When he interviewed a victim he was almost timid in his approach, going the extra mile not to intimidate or offend them. He was a St. Louisan through and through, graduating from Roosevelt High School in south St. Louis and the Navy for a four year hitch.

    After the Navy he did what most of us veterans do: come home and try to get a job. It isn't easy to find a good job, and when the police department advertises for cop recruits we all say the same thing to ourselves---"I can do that."

    Patrolman Sam Lackland was just a nice guy. He was black, and he had black political friends. All he had to do was go with the flow, and he would eventually be promoted, transferred to a downtown bureau, and given a city car to drive. But it never hurt the cause to arrest a brazen daytime rapist and burglar. It's good for the resume.

    Both of these cops knew that in any district, and at any time, there was always a chance at glory, the kind of glory that will get you a detective job downtown. The cop just has to be in the right place at the right time, and be cognizant of his surroundings and his job.

    Ron Adler desired success in the St. Louis Metropolitan Police Department more than anything else in his life, even his marriage.

    One of the interesting aspects of being in the "Wild West" seventh was the fact that it was on the boundary with St. Louis County. The city crooks and the county crooks had free reign to come and go as they pleased. The city cops and the county cops worked together at times to solve heinous crimes, but there was a political division between the county and the city.

In contrast to the St. Louis Metropolitan Police Department was the St. Louis County Police Department---two different political entities.

St. Louis City, which in the early 1900's was prosperous and thriving, while St. Louis County was just farmland with some municipalities scattered around, felt being politically connected to St. Louis County was a burden the city did not need.

The City fathers of St. Louis decided that they did not wish to be associated politically with St. Louis County, so they seceded from the county. That meant the City of St. Louis was politically speaking, on its own.

The folks in outstate Missouri wanted little to do with the City of St. Louis. Jefferson City was, and is the Capitol of the Great State of Missouri, and the only politicians praising or lobbying for the City of St. Louis were St. Lousians. Everyone else was apathetic to the city's needs.

Crime has no boundaries. The crooks in St. Louis City and St. Louis County were mostly the same. Super crooks have access to super cops. Every good crook needs, and cultivates high ranking cops. They befriend cops, and act as informants for them.

The high ranking cops get notoriety from information being supplied by crooks. The crooks get cash, contraband, and stolen booty from information supplied by high ranking cops. These symbiotic relationships between crook and cop become complicated when a cop in a district arrests one of their informants.

Telephone calls are made by the cop associate on behalf of their crooked friend. The cops at times are acting as legal defense for the arrested crooks.

These associations start out innocently. A crook comes into contact with a cop in need of notoriety. The cop is given information that leads to a good arrest. The press blows the story out of proportion, and the cop becomes a hero.

This is an affliction, much like heroin addiction. Once a cop gets glorified there is nothing that can take glory's place. The cop will do anything for another dose of glory, and the crook/informant knows it.

As a young patrolman in the seventh Ron Adler made a car stop on Delmar Boulevard. A young white woman was driving the car, alone in a predominantly black neighborhood.

Patrolman Adler questioned the woman, Yevon Dietrich as to why she was in the neighborhood. Yevon was a notorious drug dealer, and well connected to two high ranking cops in St. Louis County, Major Pete Vasel, and Captain Jack Patty.

Yevon advised Patrolman Adler that she was working on a case for the high ranking St. Louis County cops, and that if he would let her go she would give him $2000. She said, "I can make your dreams come true." Ron Adler called for his supervisor.

The supervisor arrived on scene and interviewed Yevon Dietrich. As luck would have it there was an operable call box on the corner near the car stop. The supervisor excused himself and went to the call box. Several minutes later he returned to the scene, and advised Ron to release Yvon Dietrich.

Later on in his career Ron would be subpoenaed by the Missouri Task Force on Organized Crime before a Federal Grand Jury regarding Yvon Dietrich.

Ron and Sam drove around their beat without speaking. "We could eat lunch," Ron said, looking at his watch. Sam nodded. Ron drove toward the DeBalivere Strip to a buffet lunch restaurant owned by a bookie/ friend to cops.

They solemnly went through the line, got a table, cleared

their trays, stacked them at the corner of the table for future use, and ate pasta. "What do you think?" Ron broke the silence.

"About what?" Sam replied.

"This rapist. He raped a white girl on our assigned area, in broad daylight. It's our responsibility to arrest him."

"Why are you so concerned?" Sam asked. "If this victim had been black would you be so concerned? I mean, is this victim related to you, or something?"

"No, man," Ron continued. "It's just the "what ifs". What if it wasn't a boyfriend girlfriend thing? What if there's a black guy out there intent on raping young white women? It's a scary thing. Eventually this black guy is going to start killing young white women. See what I mean? That's why I'm concerned."

"Uh, yeah, I follow you. We'll just have to wait and see if he does it again, then we should start to worry. I just hope it isn't in our area during our watch. It makes us look bad, I agree with you on that."

"And there's something else we have to consider," Ron said.

"What's that?" Sam muttered.

If this rapist continues working in our area, and we get to catch him, then we'll both get commendations for our great police work, and maybe get transferred to a downtown bureau, have a take home car, and an office with a desk. We can get out of this raggedy district with its raggedy cars and its dilapidated station house. The whole damned police department is old fashioned and worn out. You know what I mean?"

"You think we're raggedy?" Sam replied. "I don't think we're raggedy. We're not as bad as East St. Louis, Illinois. You ever seen those police cars in the eastside? Now that's raggedy. And those station houses over there. Extremely raggedy! We're modern compared to them."

Ron pondered Sam's question. "Yes. I've been over there. It's totally poor there. But compared to a lot of police departments we are raggedy. Look at our scout car---it's got hundreds of thousands of miles on it. It smells of urine and blood, and beer---it reeks of tobacco. All of the district cars are like that. The suspensions in all of the cars are shot. They don't drive down the street, they bounce down the street. So we are raggedy."

"We're the cops," Sam continued. "We're supposed to be raggedy. The people we deal with day after day are raggedy. We service the poor of the world, as cops that is. Would you expect your garbage to be picked up by a limousine?"

"I see where you are coming from, Sammy, but not all police departments are raggedy like ours. I was in Los Angeles last summer. The cops there aren't raggedy. Every cop's in shape. Their cars and uniforms are new. An L/A cop showed me his cop radio. It's got numerous channels---the cops can even speak to one another from their cars. They carry nifty little portable radios on their gun belts. And speaking of guns---they carry automatics. In St. Louis the only cops who drive new cars are assigned to headquarters. The Colonels on the Honorable Board of Police Commissioners drive brand new Buicks. So we are definitely, raggedy."

"So they've got cop toys," Sammy continued. "Their crime stats are about the same as ours. They have riots and other bullshit we don't have here. The expensive toys they have hasn't helped them one damn bit."

Sammy was in deep thought. "Ron, you were born in the city, right?"

"Yep," Ron proudly replied.

"On the night you were born did your momma get a ride to the hospital from city cops?"

"I don't know, Sammy," Ron replied. "Why?"

"My momma did. City Hospital # 2, Homer G. Phillips Hospital. I'd have been born in squalor if they hadn't given her a ride. How many pregnant women have you given a ride to the hospital?"

"Dozens," Ron replied.

"Me too. I just can't justify the hating of cops. All we do is serve poor folks. It just doesn't make sense," Sammy muttered.

"I don't follow you, Sammy. What are you talking about?"

"This damned rapist, if he really is a rapist. He's sending a message to us, the cop on the beat. He's saying, "I can rape and rob anytime I want to, and you cops can't do anything about it. Or am I just overly dissecting this crime?"

"You are overly dissecting this crime," Ron said with a laugh.

They got a tray from the bin, and stacked their dirty dishes on it, dumped the cafeteria tray, and cleaned the table they were using. It was part of the procedure for getting free lunches at the buffet. The owner didn't require that they do it; it's just cop protocol for free food.

They entered the raggedy cop detective car and drove in circles around the Skinker, Pershing, and Forest Park Boulevard area, observing, and looking at faces on the street and in passing cars. The dispatcher advised them to telephone their office. A call box was their only option.

Patrolman Ron Adler and Sammy Lackland weren't the only patrol cops who wanted to catch a burglar/rapist. Patrolman Mike Benson, and Charles Schaefer were scouring the seventh district streets looking for any black guy who minutely matched the description of Milton Brookins.

On January 31st, just two days after the rape at 5349 Pershing, they spotted a black guy walking in the 400 Block of North Union who matched the description, and had scratches on his face and hands. It was 11:50 A.M., about the time the street thieves get out onto their turf to victimize the working stiffs of the world. It all added up to the two patrolman.

The suspect, Donald Agers, was incensed that he was stopped by the patrolman while walking and minding his own business.

The patrolman interrogated him on the street, and asked him about the scratch marks on his face and hands. He advised them he had gotten into a fight with his girlfriend, Margie Watkins, on January 29th, and that she scratched him.

Donald Agers was taken to the seventh district station, and interrogated further. He was asked about the rape at 5349 Pershing on January 29th.

He denied any knowledge of any rape anywhere. The rape victim was contacted, and responded to the station. A show-up was conducted with five other men prisoners who just happened to be in the district holdover at the time.

The victim positively identified Donald Agers as the man who raped her. He was booked for Forcible Rape and Armed Robbery. Warrants were applied for at the Circuit Attorney's office and were issued.

Donald Agers girlfriend was interviewed by Patrolman Benson. She advised him that she and Agers did indeed get into a fight on January 29th, and that she did scratch him on the face, hands, and back.

Donald Agers languished in the City Jail for a couple of weeks until the identity of him by the victim was questioned by investigators for the Circuit Attorney's Office. He was eventually released, and the warrants were dismissed.

It was February 5, and Patrolman Milton Brookins was on his third day off in an eight day stretch. He had been on a mental high since raping the student on Pershing. He wanted more---it was the most exciting thing he had ever experienced.

He parked the Phantom rental on a side street near Skinker and McPherson, and walked east, casually looking at apartment houses lining both sides of the street watching and waiting for the sign of a victim.

A six unit apartment building at 5912 McPherson caught his eye. It was typical of all of the "West End" apartment houses; dark brick, straight up and down architecture, plain and functional, a building that could be in Russia, Germany, or St. Louis.

The front door had no locks on it, and no sign of a buzzer or speaker. He observed a young white woman enter the building, and he was infatuated with her. He entered the building approximately five minutes after she entered.

He had no plan, just to look for a door, and listen for a female voice inside, maybe speaking on the telephone. Or he would smell the air searching for the faint odor of perfume near the door.

He was lurking in the hallway when a man living in apartment # 1 east questioned him as to why he was in the hallway. He told the resident he was looking for a guy named John, and that he had to give him a message. The resident of apartment # 1east bought this story, entered his apartment and closed the door.

Milton focused on apartment # two, smelled the faintness of perfume, tried the door and found that it was unlocked. He walked inside and closed the door.

The victim came out of a bedroom, noticed Milton standing near her doorway with a gun pointed at her, and screamed as loudly as she could.

Milton was unnerved by the scream. Screams meant possible witnesses, and the person hearing the scream will probably telephone the police.

Milton continued to point the snub nose blue steel revolver at her. "Don't scream," he told her. "I've got the wrong apartment. I was looking for John."

Milton ran from the apartment, took the stairs down, and exited the front door. He rapidly walked to the Phantom Rental, disgusted with himself for the bungled rape attempt, and the shoddy effort.

The victim telephoned the police. Patrolman Robert Bruen in charge of Ocean seven got the call. He did a good investigation, interviewed the man in apartment # one, and got a good description of Milton Brookins.

But this was a routine assignment. Black males were always prowling around and burglarizing West End apartment buildings. It's what they did----prowl and look for something to steal. They were wanderers and gatherers just like the Neanderthals at the beginning of time.

Milton went back to targeting and following Washington University students. On the previous day he had spent the morning on the campus, walking and nodding to students with his phony book bag stuffed with old paperbacks. He blended in nicely, even though he was one of the few blacks wandering near the quadrangle.

He spied a gorgeous young white woman, light blonde hair, creamy skin, in shape, and athletic, and he followed her home to 5921 Kingsbury, walked inside of the building and saw which apartment she lived in. It was another six unit apartment building. He noted that when he viewed the young woman at the campus it appeared she had afternoon classes, which meant she would probably sleep late in the mornings, casually get out of bed and make some breakfast, and then proceed to the campus.

At 9:30 the next morning Milton was at her front door. He rang the doorbell, and she came to the door wearing a dressing gown, just as Milton had expected.

She opened the door approximately twelve inches and looked out to the hallway. She observed Milton standing at her door, and she thought she recognized him but didn't know where she had previously seen him. "Do I know you?" she asked.

"You have never seen me before," Milton replied. The victim then noticed the snub nosed 38 caliber pistol in Milton's right hand pointing at her mid-section. "I don't want to hurt you," Milton advised, "All I want is your money, let me in."

Milton then forced his way into the apartment, and closed the door. "Is the door locked?" he asked.

"Yes," the victim replied. Milton put his hand on her arm, and turned her around so that he was standing behind her. He walked her into a hallway, and the victim picked up her purse, removed a wallet from her purse, took $7.00 from it and handed it to him. He crammed the bills into his trousers pocket, and pushed her into the bedroom.

The victim placed her purse on an end table. Milton ordered her to empty the contents of the purse onto the table top, she complied. Milton rifled through the purse contents, but took nothing else from the purse. "When does your husband come home?" Milton asked.

She didn't answer him. "Does your husband have a gun?" He asked.

"No," the victim replied.

What time is your next class?" he asked.

"1:00 P.M.," she replied. She watched him as he walked around her bedroom. She didn't see the gun anymore, and she figured he stuck it into his trousers pocket.

Milton pushed her toward the bed, and stated, "Take that gown off and get on the bed." The victim had lit a cigarette while Milton was rifling her purse, and she was smoking it while Milton was milling around in her bedroom.

"Why do you want me to take off my robe?" she asked.

"I want to tie you up," he replied.

"I'm not taking my robe off," she sternly replied.

Milton grabbed her by the arm and forced her onto the bed. "Put your hands behind your back," he demanded. The victim complied.

"You see I have a knife," Milton said holding the weapon up for her to see. He pulled a cord from a lamp, cut it and tied her hands with it while kneeling on the bed. "I'm not going to hurt you. I'm tying you up so you can't call the police."

Milton rolled her onto her back, and pushed her robe around her so that she was nude. He played with her breasts, climbed off of the bed, and undressed. He held his penis in his hand while she watched him.

"Have you ever seen one this big before?" he asked. "Is your husbands this big? Look at it," he ordered her. "It's nine inches long."

"If you are going to rape me please remove the Tampax I'm wearing, I'm on my period," the victim asked. Milton removed it and tossed it onto the bedroom floor. He went to a dresser and obtained a sock and a shirt. He stuck the sock into her mouth and tied it with the shirt. He mounted her and entered her vagina. He had sex with her for several minutes, then said, "Are your hands hurting? Do you want me to remove the cord?" She nodded, and he freed her hands. She removed the gag.

He pushed her legs upward. "You're hurting my leg," she stated, "I just had an operation on my knee." Milton looked at the scar on her right knee, got off of her and kissed the scar.

"Have you ever sucked a cock?" he asked.

"No, that would make me sick," she replied. Milton mounted her again and reached a climax. He immediately climbed off of her, pulled the sheets over her and got dressed.

"Do you have a typewriter?" he asked

"Yes, in the living room," she replied. Milton left the bedroom, went to the living room and returned with the typewriter.

"I want to type the Captain a letter," he stated. He placed paper in the typewriter and began to type:

Hi Captain Mundt:

You are an incompetent, fat fuck-head. I just fucked another white girl in your district and there's nothing you, or those other phony fuckers on the Board of Police Commissioners can do about it.

You and the rest of your dumb, fat white coppers can't catch me.

After I fucked that girl on Pershing, I walked right by Patrolman Adler who was talking on the call box. Patrolman Lackland was sitting in the police car. I looked them right in the eyes. I read their name tags as I walked by them.

You dimwitted cops will never catch me. I've been arrested in the fucked up seventh district before. You assholes couldn't hold me. I'm out and about getting white pussy, and you assholes are sitting at your desks wondering what to do. What a bunch of assholes!

Signed,

The Phantom Fucker

Milton sat down on the bed. "I've been in the penitentiary," he began. "I've raped several white ladies, and they all liked it. You liked it, didn't you?"

"Uh huh," the victim mumbled.

"Where are the keys to your car?" The victim took the keys from her end table and handed them to him. After a few minutes he gave them back to her. "I'm going to call a friend to pick me up."

Milton was silent for a couple of minutes. "This apartment house is strange, there's no alley. "I'm going to use the phone to call my friend to pick me up." Milton exited the bedroom.

The victim ran to a sun porch at the rear of the apartment, opened a window and crawled down a fire escape. She frantically ran to a neighboring house (5921 Kingsbury) and banged on their door. The neighbors let her in, gave her a blanket to cover herself and called the police.

Patrolman David Hindrichs in charge of car Mary seven received the radio call. He had heard that there was a rapist working the West End of the city, and he figured this was one of the many rape calls that were "for real".

He met the victim at the neighbor's house at 5921 Kingsbury and they walked to her apartment. Patrolman Hindrichs had his revolver out and at the ready when they entered the apartment. The door was open, but Milton was long gone.

Patrolman Hindrichs didn't play the crime scene cheaply---he called for a department photographer and a fingerprint technician.

"The rapist wore tight fitting black leather gloves during the ordeal," the victim advised.

"That's okay, we'll dust for prints anyway," he advised.

"He typed a note to your captain," the victim advised. She walked to the bedroom, retrieved the note from the typewriter and showed it to Patrolman Hindrichs.

He read it, mesmerized by the brazenness of the rapist. "I wonder how he knows Captain Barney Mundt?" he muttered. "Now, tell me exactly what happened here."

The victim gave him a blow by blow description of what had transpired. Patrolman Hindrichs made copious notes, called for his supervisor, and asked the radio dispatcher for the paddy wagon to transport the victim to the hospital.

The supervisor told the radio dispatcher to advise the patrolman to telephone him at the station. Patrolman Hindrichs telephoned the station and read the typed note written by Milton Brookins to him over the phone. "Bring the note into the captain's office when you finish up at the scene," he advised.

"Yes, sir," Patrolman Hindrichs replied. He waited for the fingerprint tech and photographer, walked the victim to the paddy wagon, locked the apartment, and drove to the station house. He went directly to Captain Barney Mundt's office.

Barney was sitting at his desk acting important, which was actually what district captains do. They have aides to do most of their work, acting important is the most critical aspect of their job.

The problem Barney had with most of the rank and file guys (black and white) was that he couldn't hide the fact he was a phony. He didn't hide the fact that he was either drunk or hung over on most days, or that he was a professional gambler who played cards with organized criminals until the wee hours, and then had to call an aide to pick him up and drive him home.

The main reason black cops didn't care for him was that he looked like an old plantation southern colonel, and slave owner. He smoked big cigars, wore flashy suits, always had a tan, and had his white hair slicked back. But like all police commanders, he had a following of sycophants ready and willing to do his dirty work.

The detective crew, headed by Detective Sergeant Chester Blancett, and consisting of Detectives George Hotsenpiller and Bobby Matthews were milling around the office while Barney Mundt acted important on the telephone

Patrolman Hindrichs entered the office. He waited for Barney to end his conversation, and then approached his desk with the note in his hand. Barney took it from him, read it and handed it to Detective Sergeant Blancett, who read it and then handed it to Detectives Hotsenpiller and Matthews. They perused it, and handed it back to Barney Mundt.

Barney's cigar was trembling as he drew from it. "I wonder if this is a cop," Barney stated. "Who uses the terminology "copper" except cops?" Barney continued. "And see how he signs Phantom Fucker in line with the left margin. It's where cops sign their reports." Barney was wiping his brow with a handkerchief. "Forcible rape? Why would a St. Louis cop resort to forcible rape?" Barney exclaimed.

"I read somewhere that rape isn't actually sexual," Bobby Matthews interjected. "It's some kind of a power play."

"Oh, really," Barney exclaimed. "I never heard that one." Barney drew deeply on his cigar then blew the smoke toward the detectives

"Sergeant Blancett, get on this and clean it up. It is making us look bad out here. Before long the damned press will be putting their noses in our business out here. We've got a good thing going for us, nobody gives a damn what goes on here in the seventh, and that's the way I like it. Get it cleaned up!" He handed the note to the detective sergeant, and he and his detectives exited Barney's office.

Detective Sergeant Blancett held a meeting with his entire staff: "Find this rapist," he ordered them.

The detectives were scouring the streets, and searching for clues. Detectives Jinkerson and Sannamon remembered a suspect they had arrested on a previous occasion that matched the description of the rapist.

They gathered the photo of the previous suspect, placed it in a group of other photos and went to the victim's residence.

The victim picked out the photo of the previous suspect. The detectives began a search for him. He was eventually found at 6041 Washington and arrested at this time.

He was transported to the seventh district station, and placed in a show-up with two other prisoners who matched the description of the rapist.

The suspect was then interviewed in the presence of the victim. He advised that he knew nothing about the rape, and he had never seen the victim before. He said he had an alibi, that he was with his girlfriend and that they were at 5968 Cates until approximately 6:00 P.M.

The rapist allegedly was wearing blue boxer style underwear. The arrested subject also was wearing blue boxers.

The detectives booked the suspect for Forcible Rape and Robbery. The Circuit Attorney's office refused the warrants. The suspect did 20 hours incarcerated in the police holdover, and was released.

6

Milton knew he had tempted fate in the "Wild West" seventh district. It was time to move his criminal activity to a new location. He chose the Central West End, just a short distance from the West End. The CWE was fashionable, near hospitals and colleges, and was predominantly white.

White women walked the streets there, shopping and eating at sidewalk cafes without fear of street crime. It was a vibrant community with million dollar homes, and a plush and fashionable shopping area.

There were fancy hotels and residence hotels around the Barnes Hospital complex which could be entered easily by anyone with a small amount of imagination.

Milton chose The Ambassador Hotel at the corner of Kingshighway and West Pine, just across the street from the world famous Forest Park---the jewel of St. Louis---the location of the 1904 World's Fair, and it was in the bloody ninth district, a place noted for strange crime.

The poor blacks mingled with the wealthy whites during the daylight. It would be rude to suspect any black of a crime against a person while the sun was out. Being racially correct was an important aspect of living in the CWE.

But when darkness fell, the CWE residents locked themselves into their palatial homes, set their burglar alarms, and did not venture outside unless it was necessary. Living in the CWE was like living in South Africa.

There were apartments as well as hotel rooms in the Ambassador Hotel. Servants had access to these rooms, and it was common knowledge in the black community that the white women who lived there often kept their doors unlocked so the servants could come and go as they pleased without disturbing the tenants.

Phantom Rapist

On February 12, at approximately 8:00 A.M. Milton entered the hotel and prowled the hallways trying doors. It had been two days since his last escapade on Kingsbury, and he was ready for action.

He found an open door on the second floor, room 205, and he entered. He called out, "anybody home?" because that's what a servant would have said. He didn't get an answer so he closed the door and started rifling drawers in the bedroom of the one bedroom apartment.

He found a white metal tie pin with a diamond, and a $20.00 bill. He stuffed them in is trousers pocket and waited.

The victim, a white lady forty six years of age, opened the door to her apartment and walked into the bedroom. She observed that her dresser drawers had been removed and rifled, and she walked back into the living room to call for the hotel staff, thinking that a servant had stolen from her.

Milton was waiting for her in the living room. He struck her with his fist in the right shoulder, knocking her to the floor before she could see him or scream for help. She looked up at him as he jumped on top of her, tearing at her clothing.

Milton tore her blouse off and grabbed at her bra, scratching her skin in the process. The victim fought back, screaming and fighting, kicking with her feet as she lay on the floor. Milton got off of her and ran out of the apartment door. The victim gathered herself and called the police.

An old salt patrolman, Walter Otten, in charge of car John 9 responded to her apartment. Walter was soured to the world, and to ninth district rape calls. He'd handled scores of them in the bloody ninth district, in fact he'd been handling them for more than 20 years. In his mind, the victim was always in the wrong.

He took the information provided to him from the victim,

and walked out. It was just another attempted rape call in the CWE, nothing to be concerned about.

    Milton left the hotel for approximately five hours, then returned. He again prowled the halls trying doors, and then stopped at room # 223 and tapped on the door.
    The victim, white female twenty one, said, "Who's there?"
    Milton responded, "I was sent up from downstairs to do something in your room." The victim opened the door for him.
    Milton had a blue steel revolver in his hand and he pointed it at her face. "If you do everything I tell you to do you won't get hurt." He backed her into the apartment, closed and locked the door, and engaged a safety chain lock. "Give me all of your money," he ordered her." She scurried around the apartment and came up with $20.00 in five's.
    Milton prodded her with the revolver, and then took a pocket knife from his trousers pocket and stuck the revolver into the same pocket. He opened the knife and held it up for her to see. "If you don't do what I tell you to do, I'll cut your face up."
    "Please, sir," she pleaded, "You've got all of my money, please leave my apartment. Please don't hurt me."
    "You do what I say and I won't hurt you," Milton repeated. "Take off all of your clothes," he ordered. The victim complied.
    A servant tried to enter the apartment, but the chain lock prevented her from entering. The servant then closed the door.
    Milton removed his clothing, and then ordered the victim to go into the bedroom, and to get on the bed. Milton followed her into the bedroom, got on top of her and inserted his penis into her vagina. Milton did not ejaculate.

He climbed off of her, clothed himself and said, "Pose in the mirror for me." She stood in front of the mirror on the bathroom door and did poses for him as he instructed her. He felt on her body as she posed.

He ordered her to sit on a chair in the bedroom. He would periodically go to the apartment door and listen and then he would come back to the chair and stare at her. After approximately thirty minutes he said, "Get back on the bed and let's screw."

Milton removed his trousers but left his shirt and jacket on, and again raped the victim. He did not ejaculate. "Get up, and go into the bathroom," he ordered her. "If you continue to remain quiet you will not get hurt."

The victim went into the bathroom, and Milton closed the bathroom door. A short time later the victim heard a light switch flip on in the living room. A servant opened the bathroom door and observed her. She quickly dressed and went to the hotel staff to tell them what had transpired.

Patrolman Royce Boone and Raymond Prinzen in charge of cars Charles nine and Ida nine received the radio call. The second assault in the same day and on the same floor at the Ambassador Hotel was big news. Milton had shaken the bloody ninth district in the same manner he had disturbed Captain Barney Mundt in the "Wild West" seventh.

Milton was long gone by the time the ninth district cops arrived. Milton just lived ten minutes away in Laclede Town. He was probably enjoying a home cooked meal as the victim was being conveyed to City Hospital # one in the back of a stinking paddy wagon.

Milton had gotten a little sloppy. He placed his horn rimmed sun glasses on a living room chair, and left them there. They were conveyed to the department laboratory to be dusted for fingerprints. But this act was to no avail; no prints recovered due to contaminated surfaces.

7

On February 14, Milton had been prowling around the apartment building at 4921 West Pine looking for a potential victim. He had scored big just two days earlier at Kingshighway and West Pine, and he liked the area.

West Pine near Euclid had modern apartment houses, made of brick and glass. The residents of this part of the City of St. Louis were extremely liberal and were hesitant to telephone the police about black people prowling around their neighborhoods.

The victim had just gotten off of work at the plush and fashionable Chase Park Plaza Hotel at 212 N. Kingshighway where she worked as a desk clerk. It was the hotel where presidents and celebrities stayed when they visited St. Louis.

She fit the mold for Milton, just twenty years old, cute and in shape, and she lived alone in the CWE. Milton had seen her at the hotel while he was searching for possible victims, and he was smitten with her.

He made note of her hours at the front desk, and followed her home on a previous day. He was waiting for her when she came home from work at 4:20 P.M. after the day shift.

The victim took the stairway up to her apartment on the seventh floor and placed the key in the door. Milton approached her from the rear and grabbed her around the neck with his left arm.

He showed her his snub nosed revolver and then placed it at her temple, "Don't scream, and don't make any loud noises," he advised her. He pushed her into the apartment, and closed and locked the door.

"Where's your money?" Milton asked.

"I only have a few dollars," the victim said. She dug into her purse and came up with $8.00. She handed it to him and he stuffed it.

"Is there anybody else in the apartment?" Milton asked.
"No," she replied.

Milton pushed the victim down the hallway toward the bedroom. He looked into the other rooms as they walked down the hallway. Upon reaching the bedroom Milton pushed the victim onto the bed, "Take your clothes off, do it now," he ordered. The victim just stared at Milton. Milton displayed a knife and said, "I ought to cut you, take those damn clothes off."

The victim complied, and Milton tied her hands behind her back with a nylon stocking. Milton undressed, and then mounted the victim. He raped her until he ejaculated, got up and dressed.

Milton stared at the victim for several minutes then left the apartment. The victim tried to telephone the police but Milton had apparently removed the speaker part of the telephone, and took it with him. She went to a neighbor to call the police.

Patrolman John Michael Letz, in charge of car Ida nine received the radio call to the victim's apartment. John was a kind cop, but he wasn't exactly interested in the victim's story. Mike's dad was a state employee and had state political influence. Mike was in waiting for a job in the detective bureau, and this alleged rape wasn't a top priority for him.

John called a paddy wagon for a conveyance to City Hospital # 1, interviewed a couple of neighbors, and then got on with his quest for glory as a detective.

John Michael Letz's dad came through for him. He did some years in the ninth district detective bureau, was promoted to sergeant and then to lieutenant.

He was eventually assigned as the Commander of the prestigious Intelligence Unit. He ran that unit for several years, became ill and died a young man.

Milton grew fond of the bloody ninth district, and the CWE. On February 16th, at 1:50 A.M. he returned to 108 N. Kingshighway and roamed the halls looking for a victim.

He got on an elevator with a possible victim, a white lady 46 years of age. They took the elevator to the third floor, where the victim's apartment was located. Milton did not speak to her while on the elevator, but when the elevator stopped on the 3rd floor, and when the victim exited, Milton exited and followed her as she was walking to her room.

Milton said, "I've been watching you, and I'm going to have you." The victim screamed, ran to her room, entered same and locked the door, and called the police. Milton escaped without completing his mission.

Milton continued his rampage of the bloody ninth district, and the CWE. On February 17 at approximately 8:50 A.M. Milton was loitering in an apartment hallway at 4520 Forest Park Boulevard.

The victim, a white lady twenty four years old had just gotten off of work at a hospital where she worked as a nurse, and she was bone tired. She noticed Milton standing approximately fifteen feet away from her as she placed the key in her apartment door, but she didn't give him notice, and she turned her back on him as she attempted to enter her apartment.

Milton did his usual terror tactic with the gun and orders, as he pushed his way into the apartment, locked the door and stared at her. "I don't want you in my apartment, take what you want and leave," the victim said.

"Take your clothes off," Milton ordered as he held the gun in her face. The victim balked. "Take off your damn clothes and I won't hurt you," he said with the .38 pointed at her face.

The victim removed her clothing. He forced her into the bedroom. "Get on the bed. Lay on your side facing the wall," he ordered. She complied, but snuck a peek at him as he was tampering with her telephone.

Milton raped her and ejaculated, then sat around and wanted to talk with her. He referred to her as "baby", and told her he had been to prison for raping white women, and he figured that if he was going to go back to prison then he might as well rape as many white women as he could before he got caught.

He was in her apartment for three hours and raped her three times. He cut a lamp cord, and a toaster cord, and used them to bind her wrists and ankles. He stuffed her mouth with toilet tissue, and used white hospital tape to secure the gag.

Milton exited the apartment carrying her typewriter, her wrist watch, and her car keys.

The victim freed herself, went to a neighbor's apartment and telephoned a Doctor associate at Jewish Hospital. The physician responded to her apartment and then the police were notified.

Patrolman Prince Timmons in charge of car 99A responded to the scene. Prince was also a kind cop. He was a black guy who joined the department because it was a steady job. He was a religious man, and he didn't associate with any of the other coppers, black or white. He was winding his way toward a twenty year retirement, but he had a long way to go.

The supervisors didn't cut him any slack just because he was religious. They demanded arrests and traffic enforcement from Prince, and he did the bare minimum to keep the bosses happy. Car 99A was actually the paddy wagon. Laid back cops got the job of driving it.

Prince took the information from the victim, and

interviewed neighbors for any possible clues. He was scrutinized by all of the command personnel, and he knew he had better have every report correct or he would be reprimanded.

Prince went to the parking lot of 4520 Forest Park, and did not find the victim's car. Milton had stolen it. Prince conveyed the victim to a physician friend of the victim who had an office at 4511 Forest Park. The physician treated and counseled the victim.

Prince wrote a good initial report. His job was done. It was the district detective's job to identify and arrest Patrolman Milton Brookins.

Milton drove the victim's Oldsmobile until approximately 6:50 P.M. on the same day as the rape. He returned it to her by leaving it parked in a parking lot at 4488 Forest Park, just doors down from her apartment building.

A twelve year old boy observed Milton parking the car and walking away from it. He gave the usual description---Negro, 5'9 to 5'10, medium complexion about twenty five years old.

No fingerprints taken from the stolen vehicle due to contaminated surfaces.

A mini-task force of district personnel was assembled to investigate the rapes in the Central West End and the West End.

Detectives Frank Ellis, William Pietrowski, John Summers and Jadwick Lynch from the ninth district, accompanied by Patrolman Elbert Qualls from the seventh district, Dwight Wideman, and David Lowell also from the ninth, began investigating the rapes by Milton Brookins.

The mini-task force dressed in old clothing and began walking in the CWE and the West End during the daylight hours.

They also contacted rape victims and showed them a series of suspect photos. They worked twelve hour days, stopping at night fall.

Several victims identified a photo of Leamon Beene. He fit the description of the rapist. The detectives searched for him and eventually found him at his girlfriend's home at 6041 Washington.

He was arrested and placed in a show-up. Several victims identified him. Warrants were issued, and he was placed in the city jail awaiting trial.

The detectives were certain they had captured the rapist who referred to himself as the Phantom Fucker. They were strutting around the ninth district station, and patting themselves on their backs.

Detective William Hawkins of the ninth district bureau did some further investigation. He checked out the alibis that the suspect had provided to the detectives at the time of his arrest.

The suspect was working on the day and time of the rape; his supervisor verified this fact. He had also contacted his mother by telephone on several occasions, and he was with his girlfriend shortly before and after the CWE rapes.

Detective Hawkins took this information to the Circuit Attorney's Office. The Circuit Attorney withdrew the warrants and the suspect was released.

Milton was taking days off; accrued court time and overtime, time he needed to pursue his hobby of raping and robbing young white women.

On February 25th Milton was on surveillance at 326 N. Euclid in the fashionable CWE. He had previously seen a nurse walking on Euclid in the hustle and bustle of the afternoon pedestrian traffic. Milton was struck by her beauty, and decided that he would have her. He had a thing for nurses.

At approximately 3:30 P.M. he observed her walking to her apartment building, and he followed her. She got inside of the apartment and locked the door before Milton could sneak up behind her and pistol-paralyze her.

He tapped on the door, and the victim said, "Who's there?"

"I spilled some trash in the hallway. Do you have a broom I could borrow?" Milton asked. The victim had seen Milton in the building for a couple of days, and she figured he was a newly hired janitor. She opened the door, and turned to go to the kitchen to get a broom to give to him. When she returned Milton was standing inside of her apartment with a gun pointed at her face. "Stay quiet and you won't get hurt," Milton growled at her.

"I want your money," Milton stated. The victim turned to go back to the kitchen to get her purse. Milton followed her. The victim looked in her purse and came up with $2.00, which she handed to him. Milton obtained a knife from somewhere in the kitchen, and stuck the gun in his trousers pocket.

He placed the knife at her neck and ordered her into the bedroom. "Take your damned clothes off," he ordered.

"Why?" the victim asked. ""What are you going to do to me?"

"I'm not going to hurt you. I want you take off your clothes so you can't follow me when I leave," Milton replied.

"I won't follow you, just leave," the victim pleaded.

Milton placed the knife toward her face, "If you don't take off your clothes I'll cut up your face," he said. The victim removed her clothing. "Get on the bed," Milton ordered.

"What are you going to do to me?" the victim again

asked.

"I'm going to rape you. If you stay quiet I won't hurt you. I've raped over 100 white women and haven't hurt any of them." The victim got on the bed, and after a few minutes Milton got on top of her and raped her. He ejaculated and climbed off of her.

"Where do your parents live?" Milton asked.

"County," the victim answered.

"Are you going to move?" Milton asked.

"Yes," the victim replied.

"Where to?" Milton asked.

"I don't know," she replied.

Milton went to the kitchen, cut the cord from a toaster, returned to the bedroom, and tied the victim's wrists and ankles. "Don't try to free yourself for 10 minutes," Milton said. "If you do I'll know because I'll be waiting outside for a friend to pick me up." Milton left the crime scene.

The victim freed herself immediately, got dressed and went to a friend's apartment to call the police.

Patrolman Dave Northcutt in charge of car Lincoln nine got the call. Dave was a happy cop. He was proud and satisfied with the St. Louis Metropolitan Police Department, and thrilled to be assigned to the bloody ninth district.

Dave was a college student, worked all three watches and balanced his college curriculum between shift changes and night classes. He desired to be a federal agent.

The victim told Dave her story. Dave knew about the Phantom Rapist. "Did he leave a note?" Dave asked.

"No," the victim replied. Dave called for the fingerprint section to respond, and then made arrangements with the paddy wagon driver to come by and pick up the victim to convey her to City Hospital # one.

The victim thanked Dave for his kindness. Life went on for Dave. He finished college, married his sweetheart who worked in the personnel division of the police department and was eventually hired by the United States Secret Service.

Dave did enough time in the Secret Service to get a retirement and he and his family returned to St. Louis. There were other retired federal agents here working in corporate security and they helped each other at finding employment. Dave worked for Monsanto as a corporate security specialist. He died a young man.

Patrolman Dwight Wideman, one of the mini-task force officers, was intent on not giving up on the investigation. He began canvassing the businesses on Euclid, asking proprietors if they saw or heard anything suspicious before or after the rape at 326 N. Euclid.

Patrolman Wideman interviewed Ruth Altheimer, owner and operator of Rainier's Antique Shop, 331 North Euclid. She advised Patrolman Wideman that shortly before the rape, a Negro matching the description of the rapist came into her shop and watched the building across the street at 326 North Euclid, the apartment building of the victim.

She gave the same old description of Milton Brookins, and thousands of other CWE frequenters.

Patrolman Larry England, while patrolling on Maryland Plaza, noticed a black guy matching the general description of the rapist, trying doors on Maryland and on Euclid.

The suspect ran from Larry England, and was eventually captured. He refused to give any kind of a reason as to why he was trying doors, or why he ran from the police. He was conveyed to the ninth district station and booked for "peace disturbance," which is a catch-all charge for the incarceration of street people.

The suspect was interviewed by the district detectives

and subsequently released.

Ninth District Commander, Captain Harry Lee, a thinker and a military man, met with Detective Sergeant William Fitzgerald. They needed a plan to catch the Phantom Rapist; it was their responsibility. The Detective Sergeant assigned Detectives Tony Wachter and Bill Glasscock to the case. The mini-task force was a bust.

Tony Wachter was a country boy, strong, intense, and physical. Jim Glasscock was a student, always trying to learn different things. He was attending college, and he had an interest in photography. Both of these detectives loved locking up criminals, and they loved the bloody ninth district detective bureau.

There were other rapists plying their trade in the bloody ninth district. There were rapes in, and around the St. Louis University Campus, which in their minds could be the same guy as the Phantom Fucker. If not, it would still look good in the eyes of the commanders in police headquarters if someone in the bloody ninth captured them.

"I want you guys to round up all of the victims of any and all rapes in the ninth district, take them downtown and have "show-ups". Take anybody in the holdover that anywhere near fits the description or age of this damned rapist. Maybe some victim will recognize somebody," Detective Sergeant Fitzgerald ordered them.

The cop theory is: a criminal arrested for a crime in another part of the city might also be wanted for a crime somewhere else in the city, and might be cooling his heels in jail. Rapists are criminals; criminals spend most of their time incarcerated awaiting a trial on other charges. There are hundreds of arrests each day in the City of St. Louis.

Detectives Wachter and Glasscock were conveying rape victims to police headquarters to view a line-up. They used two detective cars, each with four rape victims in them. Detective Glasscock was driving through Laclede Town with a couple of victims, preparing to pick up another one. A rape victim in Glasscocks car exclaimed, "There's my damn car that the rapist stole from me after he raped me." She was pointing to an old Chevy parked in front of the laundry mat near the town circle.

Glasscock slowed, then drove past the stolen car. The detectives couldn't communicate with each other without going through the police dispatcher, so Glasscock motioned for Tony Wachter to follow him. The detectives stopped near 2912 Red Maple Walk, the residence of Milton Brookins.

Jim Glasscock exited his detective car and walked back to Tony Wachter, "Rape victim says her car, which was stolen by the guy who raped her, is parked at the laundry mat. Let's leave these ladies here and walk down to the car and see what transpires."

Detective Jim Glasscock carried a .357 magnum, and Tony Wachter carried a department .38 special, but Tony also had a sawed off .30 caliber rifle that looked like a pistol.

Before Jim and Tony could leave their detective cars, the victim who observed her car said, "There's the guy who raped me."

The detectives looked down toward the laundry mat and observed the rapist getting into the victim's Chevy. The detectives ran toward the stolen car, and as the rapist/car thief was preparing to drive away, Tony Wachter stuck the sawed off 30 caliber rifle in his face. The rapist gave up, and was taken into custody.

The detectives were hoping their suspect was the Phantom Fucker. To their chagrin, victims and witnesses could not identify him. A rapist was off of the streets, but the Phantom Rapist was still at large.

Milton Brookins was probably sitting in his town house at 2912 Maple Walk as the detectives parked their detective cars in front of his house, and ran down the street to the laundry mat. He probably got a laugh from them sticking their guns in the rapist's face, dragging him out of the stolen car, and placing cuffs on his wrists.

Milton had "torn up" the CWE and was now focusing his efforts back to the "Wild West" seventh district. It was where Washington University students were.

At 3:15 P.M. on February 26, the victim, a twenty three year old student was returning to her apartment at 5390 Pershing after classes at Washington University.

The victim was unaware that Milton had observed her on campus and had followed her home the day before. He knew her schedule, and he was waiting for her as she entered the lobby of her apartment building.

Milton had engaged an elderly resident of the building in casual conversation, and when the victim entered the lobby she observed Milton, and figured he was a friend of someone in the building, or a new resident.

The victim climbed the stairway to the third floor and noticed that Milton was also walking up the stairway. She went to her apartment, and paused as she noticed that Milton was near her.

"I'm looking for the man who lives in this apartment," Milton advised pointing to the apartment across the hall from hers. "I'd like to leave him a note. Do you have a piece of paper, and a pencil or pen I can use?"

The victim gave Milton an 8X10 note pad and a pencil, and then went into her apartment and locked the door. A short time later Milton tapped on her door and said, "I have your note pad, and your pencil."

The victim opened the door, and Milton was standing with a pistol pointing at her face. He forced his way inside of the apartment, closed and locked the door. He robbed her of $11.00, raped her, and tied her with electrical cords, then left the apartment.

The victim could not free herself from the electrical cord around her wrists. There were no neighbors at home. Nude, she walked to the lobby and then to the street before she found a large man that helped her get the cords from her wrists.

She returned to her apartment and tried to use the phone but the phone receiver had been disassembled. She found a neighbor on another floor who then called the police for her.

Two days after the rape at 5390 Pershing, Detectives Ron Sanneman, and Larry Jinkerson of the seventh district bureau, proceeded to 5390 Pershing to interview the victim, and to prepare an "Identi-Kit" composite rendering of the suspect. They asked her about a possible conversation she may have had with the suspect before, during, or after the rape.

The victim stated that during the rape, the rapist bragged about himself about how good he could perform during sexual intercourse. He asked her if her husband was as good as he was.

The detectives attempted to locate the elderly woman Milton was talking with in the lobby when the victim came home from school.

They located a Mrs. Frye, white female, seventy six. She advised them that the rapist came into the lobby and asked her if anyone in the lobby had called for a cab. There was a cab parked in front of the apartment building, and the driver was honking the horn of the cab.

Mrs. Frye advised the detectives that she did not know, and the rapist then walked to the rear of the lobby and milled around as the victim walked into the lobby, and then to the stairway. She gave the general description of a Negro man in his mid-20's.

    Several days later, Patrolman Bruce Liebsch and Joseph Robinson, in car Adam eight, received a radio call to investigate a suspicious person in the 5000 block of Westminster.
    They observed the suspect, and he ran from them. They contacted the radio dispatcher and then pursued the subject on foot. They caught him at # nine Hortense Place, in the bloody ninth district, several blocks away from the 5000 block of Westminster.
    Detective Bobby Matthews heard the pursuit, and responded to the Hortense Place address to assist the officers.
    The Patrolman and Detective Bobby Matthews felt that this subject was indeed the person who called himself the Phantom Fucker. He was arrested at this time, but he was not 25 years old, he was seventeen, and he resided at 4622 Westminster with his parents.
    Bobby Matthews asked him what he was doing in the neighborhood. He responded by stating he lived in the neighborhood, and that he was selling tickets for his church. He was searched subsequent to his arrest, and he was found to have a pocket knife in his trousers pocket. This compounded the suspicions of the officers.
    He was conveyed to the seventh district station. The victim from 5390 Pershing was summoned to come to the district station for a show-up. She responded, viewed the show-up, and stated that she could not positively identify anyone in the show-up. The seventeen year old suspect was released.

Several days after that incident, Detective Charles McCrary arrested a subject for bench warrants in the eighth district, a small, 100 % black community within the confines of the City of St. Louis, bordering the bloody ninth, and seventh districts. Charles McCrary later became the Assistant Chief of Police.

He contacted the seventh district bureau and advised the detective sergeant that the subject he arrested fit the description of the Phantom Fucker.

Detectives Jinkerson and Sanneman responded to the eighth district station, and upon viewing the suspect decided to have another show-up.

They attempted to contact all of the rape victims in the seventh and ninth districts.

The victim from 5092 Waterman was not at home.

The victim from 5912 Kingsbury was sick and confined to her bed.

The victim from 6149 Waterman was not at home.

The victim from 5390 Pershing responded to the station and viewed the show-up.

The suspect arrested by Detective McCrary refused to go out into the show-up stage and had to be physically forced to stand for the show-up.

The victim stated that the subject who refused to be seen looked like the rapist, but she couldn't be certain.

Milton couldn't stay away from the Central West End. On March 4th, at 12:30 P.M., a twenty year old receptionist was sweeping the front steps of her apartment at 4627 McPherson in the bloody ninth district.

The row style, two story brick apartment buildings take most of the block in the 4600 block. They have front entrances, street level, and stoops leading to each individual apartment.

McPherson is on the fringe of the CWE. Just two blocks north is a black ghetto; one block north is the childhood home of Tennessee Williams. But the homes on McPherson across the street from the victim's apartment building are ornate, and grand, and are a significant part of the Central West End.

Milton approached the victim in the bright winter sunlight, "Excuse me," he began, "Are there any apartments for rent in this building?" Milton chose this victim at random. He was driving around the CWE looking for potential victims and observed her. She fit his criteria—young, cute, and white.

"I don't know sir," the victim replied. "I don't work here, I just live here."

Milton pulled his pistol on her, shoved her inside of her apartment, and gave her his usual spiel, "Where's your money? Do as I say and I won't hurt you."

Milton quickly closed and locked the door, pulled the shades, and turned off all of the lights inside of the apartment. The victim gave him all of her money, $1.00.

Milton exchanged his pistol for a knife and ordered the victim into the bedroom. He held the knife to her face and said, "Take off your damned clothes, and get on that bed, or I'll cut your face up."

Victim complied, crying and pleading with him, "Please don't hurt me, sir."

"Shut up, stop crying, and do what I tell you to do," Milton replied.

Milton sat on the edge of the bed, and fondled the victim. "Would you like to hear about my rapes?" he asked. The victim was frozen in fear. "I'll tell you, I've raped white women all over this city, but my favorite places for rapes are the West End, and the Central West End."

Milton would stop talking for a while, then he would just

stare at the young woman's body, and fondle her. This went on for approximately fifteen minutes.

Milton removed his trousers, mounted the victim, and said, "Relax and enjoy this." He raped her for approximately 10 minutes, ejaculated, climbed off and sat on the edge of the bed again.

"Have you ever sucked a cock?" he asked.

"No," she replied, "And I'm not going to."

Milton placed the knife at her throat, "Yes you are." He placed his penis in her mouth. After approximately ten seconds he removed it and searched the apartment. "Get up and get dressed," he ordered her.

There was a knock at the front door. Milton pulled his pistol and pointed it at her, "Look outside and see who that is. Get rid of them if you don't want them killed."

The victim looked out of a draped window, "It's the telephone man," she replied. "My phone's been out of order." She went to the door, and without opening it she asked the repairman to come back at a later date. The repairman left. Milton tested the telephone and found that it was indeed not working.

"I want you to write me a letter," Milton said. "Do you have a pen and some paper?"

"Yes, sir," she replied. The victim went to a desk, obtained writing materials, and returned to the bedroom. She sat on the bed as Milton dictated to her:

Dear Officers:

I am writing this letter to let you know that you are pretty slow when it comes to catching me. Yes, I'm the guy known to you as the Phantom Fucker. The last letter I left for you was typed by myself on February 10th when I was at 5921 Kingsbury, 3rd floor.

Because this lady doesn't have a typewriter, she is writing the letter for me. Since then I have raped Paulette at the Ambassador Hotel on Kingshighway. Also Rhonda, the nurse at 4520 Forest Park. Also Kathy, at 326 N. Euclid, and Sandra at 5340 Pershing. Also another Sandra at the apartment building owned by the Ambassador Hotel on West Pine. I don't think Sandy reported her encounter to the police.

I also committed the one to the minister's wife who lives at 53 or 5400 Pershing when she was coming home from the laundry mat. Her first name is Betty, and her husband's name is Pete. I don't remember the exact date or last name. She promised she would not report me to the police, but I found out she did later.

I don't want those other guys you locked up to take credit for my good deeds. I have gotten many more but there are too many to remember, honestly. If you wonder why I do this, it's simply for kicks. I enjoy out smarting you slow witted cops .

Signed,

The Phantom Fucker

"You see," Milton began to the victim, "I want these cops to think I'm crazy. If they get lucky and catch me they'll send me to the mental hospital instead of jail. Understand?"

"Yes, sir," the victim replied.

Milton cut the cords from two lamps in the living room. He told her to sit on a kitchen chair. He bound her wrists and ankles to the chair with the electrical cords. He went into the bathroom and turned on the water in the sink. He returned to the victim bound to the chair, picked the chair up and carried the victim into the bathroom.

"I'm hungry," Milton said. He left the victim bound in the bathroom, and went to the kitchen. The victim heard him opening and rummaging around in the refrigerator.

Milton returned to the bathroom eating an apple. He placed his knife against her throat, "You will fail to recognize me in a police line-up, understand?" He turned and exited the bathroom, "I'm not leaving yet," he said.

The victim waited for approximately five minutes, and did not hear Milton in her apartment. She tried to free herself from her bounds but Milton had done a good job tying her. She tried scooting the kitchen chair out of the bathroom and into the living room. She slowly made her way to a window in the living room.

She tore down the drapes with her teeth, and sat in front of the window. She observed her upstairs neighbor coming up the walk towards her front door. She shouted to him, and he went to the rear of her apartment, and entered through a sliding door. He untied the victim, and then contacted the police.

Patrolman Bob Broughton in charge of car George nine received the call. Bob was a good-steady type of a cop. His life revolved around his recreation sheet, the schedule of when his days off were going to be. He would plan every day off for the entire year---fishing, hunting, drinking and relaxing were his goals in life.

He was infatuated with the bloody ninth district. Bob had career opportunities offered to him. He had passed up positions in headquarters, and in other neat and tidy specialized police units throughout the city.

"Those jobs never last," he once said. "If some politician's cousin wants my job, then I'm out looking for a new home. I'll never get the ninth again, so I'll just stay where I am." He viewed the cop job in the City of St. Louis as a political appointment, for in actuality it is.

Cops like Bob Broughton become programmed to be the journeyman, steady cop who does all of the work, and gets none of the credit. The cop job was like a hobby to him. He enjoyed seeing victims, and he was interested in their plight. Other people in misery made him feel superior.

The key to Bob Broughton's laid back lifestyle was his wife. She had a good paying job. They purchased a new house in Fenton, Missouri, and Bob didn't have to join the "rat race" of working secondary or attending college to possibly better himself in life.

Bob arrived on the scene and was met by the victim. He immediately sized her up; young naive and attractive.

She told Bob her story. Bob surveyed the scene, collected her panties, and instead of making her ride in the back of a paddy wagon, he conveyed her to City Hospital # one in his scout car.

Bob wrote a good report, and went on to his next assignment. His job was done. It's the way he wanted it.

Eventually Bob's outlook on life affected his marriage. His wife divorced him and took the house they lived in. Bob had purchased a little cabin in the boonies that he had used to escape reality, and to stay in while he fished, when he was still married.

He kept the cabin and lived in it while he was a cop in the "Wild West" seventh district. He had gotten transferred out of his beloved ninth district, a fate he dreaded.

The fishing cabin was not in the confines of St. Louis County, and city cops were mandated by state law to live in either the city proper, or St. Louis County.

Bob's immediate supervisor knew that Bob did not meet the guidelines pertaining to residency and he browbeat Bob for this.

Bob was not one to take close scrutiny, so he retired early

thinking he could survive in the little cabin and fish his life away. He couldn't! He died a young man.

The victim of the rape on McPherson contacted the ninth district detective bureau, and advised that the person who had raped her left a pair of dice on a bookcase in her living room.
Detectives Dan Kirner and Ed Egenriether responded to her apartment and seized the pair of dice. They conveyed them to the department laboratory and had them dusted for fingerprints. Prints not available due to contamination.
Detective Tony Wachter desired another interview with the victim on McPherson. He went to her apartment to ask her if the rapist said anything to her that could be useful to his investigation.
She advised Detective Wachter that during sex with her, the rapist advised her that he had raped several other women. He told her that he had tried to rape a forty year old woman at the Ambassador Hotel, and that she was "well stacked".
He told the victim that the woman at the Ambassador put up a good fight, and that she got away from him. He told her he was going to go back and "get some of her".

On March 5, Detective Bobby Matthews arrested a suspect pertaining to the rape at 5390 Pershing. The victim tentatively identified a photo of the suspect. During the show-up, the victim identified him.
He was booked for Forcible Rape, and C.C.W. Knife. Warrants were issued by the Circuit Attorney's office, and the suspect was confined at the City Jail.
After checking the alibis of the suspect, he was released, and the warrants were withdrawn.

8

Milton was back at work in the Carondelet District. The press had gotten all of the information available through police sources pertaining to the Phantom Fucker, now referred to in the press as the Phantom Rapist.

It was fodder for conversation in all of the police districts, but especially in the Lilly white Carondelet district. Blacks raping whites was unthinkable. Many white cops commented on what they would do to the rapist if they caught him. Punishment ranged from castration, to torture, to public hanging.

Captain Harry Lee in the bloody ninth was showing more concern; drastic measures were in store to catch the Phantom Rapist. He again had meetings with the Detective Sergeant, William Fitzgerald, and assured him if he, and his crew of detectives could clean these rapes up there would be some promotions coming their way. Commanders assume that every cop is silently seeking promotion.

"It might be a city copper," Harry Lee said. "Check with your detectives, and see if any of them know of any white cops who might have suspicions."

"Yes, sir, Captain," the old sarge replied. The sarge charged his men with the task of finding and identifying any black, city coppers who might fit the description of the Phantom Fucker. It was a witch hunt, and as in all witch hunts, innocent people become victims.

Patrolman Myron Johnson was a light skinned and handsome black man, and he frequented white bars in the bloody ninth district. He also dated white women. This alone made him suspect in the eyes of the white cops.

He reasonably fit the description of Milton Brookins, but so did 10,000 other St. Louis residents. Myron frequented

O'Connell's Pub on North Boyle at Olive Boulevard. It was in the slowly dying Gaslight Square nightclub district.

The owners of O'Connell's Pub hated city cops, but for some reason they liked Patrolman Myron Johnson. He sat at the bar almost every night, and drank with the long haired dope smokers who frequented the place. He also dated some of the waitresses and customers. He was a fixture there.

The area cops, and the bloody ninth district detectives observed Myron on several occasions. He wasn't assigned to the bloody ninth---he had an office job in headquarters. That meant he had his evenings free, and most of his weekends.

Detective Tony Wachter still had blood in his eye, and the scent of a rapist in his nostrils. He had observed Myron on many occasions, and had even stopped him on the street and searched him. Myron advised Tony that he was a city cop and Tony Wachter backed off. But Tony never forgot him.

Tony advised Detective Sergeant William Fitzgerald that Patrolman Myron Johnson had a strong resemblance to the Phantom Rapist, and that he frequented CWE, bars West End bars, and dated white women.

"Get his photo in civilian attire from personnel. Show it to some victims, and maybe some witnesses and let's see what happens," the sarge said.

Tony got right on it. But Tony wasn't inspired by the promise of a promotion. He just enjoyed being a district detective in the bloody ninth district. It had diversity: rich people, poor blacks, businesses, and a plethora of interesting crime. The rapes by the (now with a new name) Phantom Rapist intrigued him.

Tony got together a group of twenty mug shot photos of ninth district criminals and inserted Patrolman Myron Johnson's photo among them. He contacted the young nurse victim, Kathy from 326 N. Euclid, met with her and showed her the photos.

When the victim came to the photo of Myron Johnson she stated, "This is the man who raped me."

One of Kathy's neighbors observed Milton as he was leaving Kathy's apartment after raping Kathy. She observed the photos, and picked out Myron Johnson as the possible same man.

The photos were shown to victim Gail from 4627 McPherson. "When she got to Myron Johnson's photo she said, "This looks like the man who raped me, but I can't be certain."

Victim Diana from 108 N. Kingshighway viewed the photos and said, "This looks like the man who raped me, but I can't be certain," when she came to Myron Johnson's photo.

Detective Tony Wachter decided to have an official line-up at police headquarters. He contacted Assistant Circuit Attorney Melroy B. Hutnick, and advised him of the line-up.

Lieutenant Fred Grimes, a black man who if he hadn't been a police officer would have been classified as a serial killer, went to O'Connell's Pub, and observed Myron Johnson at the bar.

Lieutenant Grimes had probably killed more street criminals than Chief of Detectives Lieutenant Colonel John Doherty. But he wasn't referred to as Back-shot Fred. He murdered his victims by looking them in the eye and shooting them with a twenty gauge sawed off shotgun.

Lieutenant Grimes primarily killed black street crooks. The white establishment loved him for it. He was praised by the good old boy regime for his so-called-dedication. He was promoted several times, and then reduced in rank for something stupid, like a procedural violation. The good old boys would then turn their backs on Fred. He was only loved when he was killing.

It didn't take Fred Grimes long to figure that he would be praised and stroked if he killed blacks--- so he did.

Lieutenant Grimes advised Patrolman Myron Johnson that he was ordering him to accompany him to the ninth district station. Myron went willingly with Lieutenant Grimes.

At the station, Captain Harry Lee advised Myron that his picture had been identified in connection with a crime which had occurred in the ninth district, and that he would be conveyed to the Inspectors Office.

Myron was conveyed to headquarters by several officers, including Lieutenant Fred Grimes. Major Joseph Kraft, Acting Inspector of Police, advised Myron that his picture had been positively identified by two victims, and one witness, and tentatively identified by another pertaining to a rape case. He was read his constitutional rights.

Myron Johnson was placed in a line-up with six other black male subjects. Assistant Circuit Attorney, Melroy B. Hutnick, responded to the line-up.

Melroy B. Hutnick was the Chief Warrant Officer for Circuit Attorney Corcoran. He could have assigned another assistant to view the line-up, but he chose not to relegate this assignment to one of his assistants. The ninth district cops were prepared to do anything in their power, even by coercing the victims if need be, to get clean-ups for the Phantom Fucker rapes in the bloody ninth district.

What they were not aware of was that, Melroy knew the ins and outs of the St. Louis Metropolitan Police Department. His dad had been a St. Louis cop. He was raised on stories about the cop job.

If all of the I.Q.'s in the room were added together they still could not come near to Melroy's. He was a no non-sense guy. There was no gray area for him.

The first victim to view the line-up was victim Gail, from

McPherson. Each subject was ordered to walk forward and state his name, address, and age, and then turn to the right and then to the left, and then turn around for a back view.

Victim Gail from McPherson said, "I'd like the number four man to smile." It was Patrolman Myron Johnson. He was ordered to smile. Victim Gail said, "Yes, I think it's the number 4 man."

The witness from North Euclid, identified the # two man who she observed leaving nurse Kathy's apartment on N. Euclid. He was not Myron Johnson.

Nurse Kathy from North Euclid stated, "The number four man looks like the man who raped me but I can't be certain. Can I hear him talk?"

Myron was ordered to step forward and say, "Do as I say and I won't hurt you," and, "Don't use the phone for ten minutes."

Myron obeyed his commanders, and made the statements.

"His voice doesn't sound like the man who raped me," Nurse Kathy said.

Victim Diana from 108 North Kingshighway viewed the line-up. "The number four man looks like the man who raped me. Can I see him walk fast?" Myron was ordered to walk fast back and forth on the stage, so he did.

"It looks like the man, and he walks like the man, but the man who raped me had shinier hair."

After the line-up was completed Circuit Attorney Melroy B. Hutnick stated that his office would take no action against Patrolman Myron Johnson at this time with the information that was available. Myron Johnson was not booked for the alleged charges.

Mass murderer Lieutenant Fred Grimes gave Myron a ride back to his hang-out bar, O'Connell's Pub. Myron was greeted with open arms by the cop-hating, dope-smoking hippies.

Myron eventually resigned from the St. Louis Metropolitan Police Department and took a job as an investigator for the State of Missouri.

The strong country boy, Tony Wachter, married a lady with means and moved to one of the western states. He had a 20 year retirement from the police department. He telephoned his buddies frequently and told them mostly what he did all day was ride horses in the desert.

The mass murderer Lieutenant Fred Grimes was offered Chief of Police jobs in the area, including the infamous East St. Louis, Illinois chief position but he turned them down.

Everyone knew what Fred Grimes' specialty was, killing street criminals. He was a possible hired gun and maybe Fred realized that fact. Fred's real claim to fame was that he only killed black street criminals. That fact alone held him in high esteem within the confines of the white controlled criminal justice system.

But Fred Grimes wasn't only feared by street criminals----he was also feared by cops. The cops who had the misfortune of working for Fred feared him and hated him.

Fred would shout at his men and he was a threatening man, large and intimidating. When arrests were made Fred would impose on the cops, shouting and berating them. If a supervisor, sergeant, would intervene, Fred would shout, "I'm the head motherfucker in charge here."

Fred knew he was a sick man and he made arrangements to have his body donated to the St. Louis University Medical School. He died of a massive heart attack. He was a young man.

Rumors surrounded his decision to donate his body. Cops spread the rumor that Fred's gargantuan carcass was hanging from a meat hook in a reefer at the St. Louis University Hospital. Enemy cops went to the medical school, let themselves inside and allegedly viewed Fred hanging on a hook. They spat on his carcass and cursed him. Wronged cops never forgive.

Melroy B. Hutnick resigned from the Circuit Attorney's Office and opened a law office in Belleville, Illinois. He is still practicing law there.

District detectives in the bloody ninth and the "Wild West" seventh were crisscrossing each other visiting rape victims and showing them photos of rape suspects.

Most victims picked out a suspect from the photos. If there was a resemblance, then they would point to the resembling suspect and say, "That's the guy who raped me".

The detectives would go helter-skelter to find and incarcerate the possible suspect. But after show-ups, the victims could not identify the real Phantom Fucker.

One subject was incarcerated in the City Workhouse due to an identification made by a victim. She later recanted and the suspect was released.

There was a drawing made by the department composite artist depicting the image of the Phantom Rapist. All of the city cops had one, even the Carondelet district cops. It was passed out at roll call; even Milton Brookins was issued a composite image.

District cops were going from district roll calls to district hangouts looking for the rapist, if he was indeed a city cop. But they limited their search to the north districts where most of the black city cops were assigned. No one came to the Lilly white Carondelet police district looking for Milton Brookins.

A lady bartender in the Central West End called the police because a black guy came into her tavern and ordered a beer. She was suspicious of the guy because he looked like the guy in the composite drawing.

"The Phantom Rapist was here," she advised the responding officer. "He stood right where you are standing and he drank a Falstaff. He was real spooky, he kept staring at the white women patrons and he scared my customers. His hand was on the bar, right there," the bar-lady advised."

The responding cop seized the Falstaff beer bottle, and the glass the possible suspect drank from. He had the fingerprint man come into the bar and dust the bar for prints, then conveyed the beer bottle and the glass to the department laboratory for possible fingerprints.

The witch hunt didn't cease.

9

Patrolman Ron Adler, like so many other city cops had an itinerary. To city cops an itinerary is a little green worm living inside of their brains telling them that they should have rank and prestige, and that they are more intelligent, worldly, and reverent than the other cops.

The worm in most cases is the cop's enemy. It causes us to do and say stupid things, to assume, and imagine, and to make attempts at heroism. The worm never helps us.

Ron's worm was telling him that he should be in a downtown detective bureau, maybe the prestigious Burglary/Robbery section of the Bureau of Investigation.

But to be assigned to that glorified unit of law enforcement meant being friends with the Chief of Detectives, Lieutenant Colonel John Doherty.

Ron had never met Chief of Detectives Doherty but he had a friend who was assigned to the unit, Detective Al Parton, and he was one of Doherty's most trusted underlings.

John Doherty had a huge reputation. Young cops would try to sneak into his offices late at night just so they could relieve themselves in his private toilet. It was a badge of honor to be able to say, "I shit in John Doherty's toilet." One young cop got a tattoo stating, "I shit where Colonel John Doherty shits."

Like gunslingers in the old west, Jesse James, Bat Masterson, Doc Holliday, they were all back shooters. Doherty was no different.

Doherty came into the police department when shooting and killing the bad guys was an acceptable trait. The problem is, and was, how does a cop differentiate between the bad guys who deserve killing from the bad guys who don't?

Doherty had the ability to make these split second decisions. In his mind, if a criminal turned and ran from him then he deserved to die from a bullet in the back.

Doherty shot so many people in the back that the criminal element nicknamed him "Back-shot John". Doherty's kids would get into fights after school because Doherty shot and killed one of their classmate's dads. The crook lore was that it was almost always from a back-shot.

The wealthy businessmen in the city revered John Doherty, and he climbed the ladder of rank within the police department.

Doherty had a membership to Norwood Hills Country Club, played golf with his best buddy, and secondary employer, trucking magnate Eugene Slay, and the elite of the region. He told them cop stories at the nineteenth hole, and was the Master of Ceremony at their residences.

By all appearances Colonel John Doherty was a success story in the river city of St. Louis, Missouri. He was a celebrity cop.

Detective Ron Adler pined for a transfer to Doherty's band of personal cops. But there was a problem looming for Ron. The lady he had let go a year or so earlier, the dope dealing lady, burglar and informant for St. Louis County Police Officers Major Pete Vasel and Captain Jack Patty, had been arrested, and was being kept incognito, spilling her guts to the feds.

It's what criminals do, inform on cops. There's no honor among thieves. She told the feds that she and a county police sergeant who had left the force planned a burglary of the S.F. Durst Company in Maryland Heights, Missouri.

The burglary was "cleared" by higher ups in the county police department in return for the arrest of a burglar. She said that in exchange for information she was to give to police about the intended burglary, drugs stolen from the warehouse would be given to her to sell.

The original three burglars Dietrich had enlisted to do the burglary for her failed to show up, so she contacted two other burglars, Paul Williams, and Larry Smith to help her.

When Williams and Smith emerged from the warehouse, Vasel, and Patty were waiting for them. They ordered them to "halt," Williams did and was arrested, Smith fled into some nearby woods, dropping a large quantity of drugs.

Dietrich was a good informant, and a smart one. She kept tape recordings of conversations between the cops, crooks, and herself.

During one of the debriefings Dietrich told the feds that she bribed a seventh district patrolman, Ron Adler, by giving him $232.00 to let her go when she had a large amount of drugs in her vehicle.

Secret debriefings are never secret for long. Information always leaks out of these closed door meetings. The Chief's office soon got word of the alleged bribe of Patrolman Ron Adler.

In any other business, and in most other police departments, a bribe accusation would be a black mark on the cop's reputation. But instead of a black mark the accusation, true or false, was a feather in the "cop hat" of Ron Adler.

Detective Al Parton went to Lieutenant Colonel Doherty and praised his friend Patrolman Ron Adler. He told him Ron was a stellar cop, and a guy who could be trusted, and that Ron desired to be transferred under Doherty's command.

Doherty was a politician as well as a killer cop. He took Detective Al Parton's recommendation under advisement.

As luck would have it, Colonel Doherty's country cabin on Dardenne Creek in St. Peters, Missouri was damaged by flood waters from the creek.

Al Parton knew that Ron was good with a hammer and a saw. He arranged for a meeting with Lieutenant Colonel Doherty, and he and Ron at the flooded cabin.

Ron surveyed the damage. "Can you fix it?" John Doherty asked.

"Yes, sir," Ron happily replied.

"I'd like to have another room added on, and a gazebo. And a brick barbeque would be nice. Can you do that?"

"Yes, sir," Ron replied. The meeting was a success, but Ron's transfer depended on how quickly he could rehab Lieutenant Colonel Doherty's flood ravaged cabin. Ron got right to work on the project, spending all of his off time demolishing and rebuilding the little cop royalty getaway.

Ron was off of the street. Instead of catching the cop who was raping and robbing, Ron was pursing his hobby of trying to better his position in the St. Louis Metropolitan Police Department.

In ancient Rome a soldier was required to swear an oath of allegiance to his general. The Latin word for this is Sacramentum. It's the same today. Ron was swearing his allegiance to Lieutenant Colonel John Doherty.

He started by visiting seventh district hardware stores. He ran a tab, and attempted to get building materials at a discount. "It's for Chief of Detectives Lieutenant Colonel John Doherty," he would tell the merchants. His country home flooded, and I'm rebuilding it for him.

He always got a discount, and some of the merchants gave him free building materials. "Tell the chief I donated to his cause," they would say.

Some would say, "You mean the cop who exterminates the vermin from this town?"

Ron would counter, "Yeah, that's him. He's always looking out for the small businessman. He's an honest citizen's friend."

Ron borrowed a pick-up truck from a friendly cop buddy, and began the chore of demolishing the walls that were too far gone from the flood in Chief of Detectives Doherty's little country home.

He knew contractors, and while on duty he would visit them and ask for advice on "how to" work on complicated restoration projects. The contractors were always willing to give advice to the local cops.

Advice doesn't cost anything, and maybe someday the contractor would need a favor, like getting a speeding ticket fixed, or getting a relative out of jail.

When Ron got stumped, or was in need of help, Detective Al Parton would assist him. Al was good for getting building materials at little or no cost for the project. He had rental property and did his own carpentry work.

Occasionally Chief Doherty would show up at the restoration project to see what progress was made. He would watch Ron toiling, point with his cigar at some changes he desired, crack a few jokes, and then drive back to the city in his big black commander Buick.

By being a shooter, and a killer, John Doherty had the city and its cops at his disposal. He was cop royalty personified. Ron worked feverishly on the interior of the flood damaged cabin during the cooler months.

On an eight day stretch he cleared the cabin of all of the ruined wood and flooring and installed new wood. The building of a new room was a challenge, but Ron chipped away at it one day at a time during his days off.

He had never built a brick barbeque, but he got the brick for nothing and stacked them where Lieutenant Colonel Doherty desired the barbeque.

He had months of work to do before he got to the barbeque, but he worked like a dog. If Ron ever finished the project, Lieutenant Colonel John Doherty would be elated,

Ron would get downtown detective status, and be one of Doherty's boys. That was all that mattered.

But there was a fly in the ointment, there always is in the cop/crook business. Ron was, most of the time, using his own money for the project. Things were getting tight at the home front. Ron's wife started balking at the expenditures, and Ron was either working at the seventh district, or working on John Doherty's country cabin. It caused a rift that never healed.

Cops can forgive and forget; cop's wives cannot. The wives of cops are in a perfect vantage point to observe the negative impact the job has on their loved ones, and they despise the cop job.

The job invades the soul of the cop. It is the challenge of ambition, not money, for the job doesn't pay enough for a cop's wife to stay at home and raise the kids. The wives must have gainful employment.

They watch as their loving, good natured, fun loving, honest husbands mutate before their eyes into sycophants, pilferers, servants for the royalty of the department, and liars.

At first the wife blames herself, then after some soul searching she blames the police department in general. But as she continues to search for something or someone to hate for her husband's indiscretions, she focuses on cop royalty like Lieutenant Colonel John Doherty.

They are the ones the younger cops learn from. But they don't learn good attributes. They learn thievery, adultery, boozing and cigar smoking. The rule of thumb is, "If Chief of Detectives, Lieutenant Colonel John Doherty, does it then it must be alright, and I'm going to do it."

It is one of the reasons cops get so many days off. The cop wife gets to take her husband back from the cop job. During a 21 day vacation the cop almost becomes human again. The wife does her best to breast feed the small minded cop back to the reality of life, "Happy wife, happy life."

But it doesn't last. After one week back at work the cop goes back to his old ways---drinking, smoking cigars, acting-important, and worshiping losers.

For Ron, there was no free time. He was either working at the seventh district and dreaming of capturing the Phantom Rapist with his partner and buddy Sammy Lackland, or he was rebuilding John Doherty's country cabin.

The cop wife eventually comes to a crossroads in their marriage, but there is a dilemma looming: if she leaves him, he won't have enough money to survive. The little bungalow in the Carondelet District will be foreclosed on, and they will both be out of a place to live.

Then she comes to the realization of the cop job---it really isn't a job the cop is supposed to be able to live off of. The job is meant to be a stepping stone toward greater things.

The city doesn't desire non-ranking cops to be career men. The city pays for education benefits for their employees. Cops can go to school for free. The master plan is for the cop to become educated, give the city five years of the cop's blood, and then move on.

It is how the system was designed to work. That way there will always be ambitious young cops on the streets of St. Louis eager to do the right thing for the politically correct commanders who sit in their offices and flirt with their secretaries, smoke big cigars and drive big cars.

But there was another way for success without attending college---become friends with a commander (like John Doherty) preferably one who has influential friends outside of the police department, and also become friends with the influential targets.

The pension fund has a twenty year retirement for cops who wish to take it. It's retirement with forty percent of the cop's pay, but it's something for the cop who needs to get out, and investigate a new career field for himself.

The green worm in Ron's head told him to take this tack. Ron pushed himself, sacrificed his family life and his health to garner friendship from Lieutenant Colonel John Doherty. It was a gamble, a long shot, but Ron was not deterred.

Ron and his buddy Sam Lackland were detached to the seventh district detective bureau to work on the Phantom Rapist case. Both were elated; they had arrived.

Colonel John Doherty led a life of prestige. After retiring from the police department, he went to work for Anheuser Busch. He stayed there until death. He knew when the grim reaper was coming for him. He wanted his legacy to live on, so he married a young woman, a waitress who he met in one of his haunts.

The widow of a police veteran gets a third of his pension upon his death. This young waitress will be, and has been reaping the benefits of being kind to good old Lieutenant Colonel John Doherty. John has been deceased for decades and the pension board sends her a check every month.

10

Patrolman Milton Brookins had just begun a 10 day stretch on the night watch in the Carondelet Police District. He once loved the night watch. It gave him an opportunity to visit his hillbilly girlfriends in the district.

Radio assignments were sparse in Carondelet in the winter. A cop could go all night with just a few radio calls. Milton had plans for this night watch, he was going to visit both of his girlfriends on each eight hour shift, one at the beginning, and one near the end.

But Acting Sergeant Harry Freeman had other plans for Patrolman Milton Brookins. Carondelet citizens had been calling the district commander and complaining about a black cop driving around the district with young white girls in his police car.

The commander ordered Harry Freeman to investigate the allegation. Black men and young white girls were not supposed to associate, cop or not.

Milton showed up for roll-call, and was advised that he was going to have a riding partner. A riding partner in Carondelet meant a white riding partner. Milton was perplexed at this information.

He knew that everything he said or did would be repeated verbatim to Acting Sergeant Harry Freeman, and then given to the district commander in a memorandum.

Milton went along with the program. It was a long first night back to work. The white cop drove around the district while Milton sat silently in the passenger seat. The white cop tried to engage Milton in conversation but Milton mostly sat mute.

Finally the cop got Milton to talk about his family. Milton spoke lovingly about his infant daughter but that was it. The age old cop conversation about past, present, and future was left hanging.

The next morning the white cop went to Acting Sergeant Harry Freeman. "I don't want to ride with him anymore, he won't communicate with me, it's like riding with a "stiff'---get me out of this."

Harry changed the work sheet---Milton was now back to riding in a one man car. He was free to pursue his hobby, young white girls. But he knew Harry Freeman was curious about him, curious enough to place him under surveillance.

Milton realized that in order to make his sexual desires a reality, he needed to have Acting Sergeant Harry Freeman as his friend. Harry had tried to befriend Milton but Milton rebuffed him.

Milton thought back to Mill Creek Valley. The old folks schooled the young'uns on the way of the white man, and how a Negro could "play" him and get what he or she wants.

It happened in slavery, the smart Negroes got to live in better houses, eat better food (high off the hog) and not work as hard as the insolent slaves. Milton knew how to talk, and he had a great smile when he wanted to flash it. The "white devil" would think that he truly likes and admires him, and Acting Sergeant Harry Freeman would get off of his back.

Traffic violations were the way to Acting Sergeant Harry Freeman's heart. Traffic violations had meaning in the St. Louis Metropolitan Police Department. They gave stature to the cops. They had multiple meaning: they meant the cop on the beat was diligent, that safety was paramount and they gave stature to the higher ranking cops.

Traffic enforcement was the stalwart of the criminal justice system. If a district had good traffic enforcement then they had good law enforcement. And one of the most important virtues of traffic enforcement was, the Acting

Sergeant, or the watch commander, or any other cop in the City of St. Louis, had the authority to go to the prosecutor and tell him, or her, that the violator receiving the traffic summons was a reliable informant and he/she should be spared a day in court or a fine. Everybody was a winner with traffic enforcement.

Milton sat up on a red light on South Broadway at Bates. He wrote a couple of summonses, got called a "niggar" a couple of times, and then called for Acting Sergeant Harry Freeman to meet him. The met up on a service station parking lot on Gravois, and pulled up to one another's cop car, driver's window to driver's window.

Milton flashed his smile and handed Harry Freeman the two summonses. Harry was elated. In his mind these summonses meant a turning of attitude for Patrolman Milton Brookins. Harry instantly liked Milton, and their friendship blossomed. Milton was now free to do what he wanted while on duty.

Milton drove by his hillbilly girlfriend's house. It was late and cold, but Milton was determined. There was a light on at the little apartment he rented with one of the girls. Milton parked his scout car on an adjoining street and walked to the apartment. He had a key, it was partially his apartment.

He used the key and entered. His favorite hillbilly girlfriend had a male guest in their apartment. Milton stood and glared at them as they sat on the couch, drinking beer, smoking cigarettes, and watching "Gunsmoke" reruns.

"What the fuck's going on here?" Milton asked. The hillbilly girl, and the hillbilly man were surprised. The man stood, Milton shoved him in the chest causing him to sit back down on the couch.

Milton took account of him; dirty, bearded, body-odor, about Milton's age, with a beer gut. The apartment was filled with smoke, stale beer bottles littered the table.

"I wasn't expecting you," the hillbilly girl began. "You haven't been here in a week, I figured you'd had enough of me and you wasn't coming back."

"I'm paying for half of this fucking place," he said while motioning with his hand. "Whose this motherfucker?" he asked while pointing at the hillbilly man.

He's just like you, Milt, he's just a friend, that's all. He comes by and visits me from time to time."

"You wearing my ring?" Milton asked.

"Yes, I'm wearing it," she replied.

"You're dating a niggar?" the hillbilly man exclaimed pointing his thumb at Milton as if he was hitchhiking.

Milton ignored the slur. "I'm not paying anymore rent on this place. We're finished!" Milton stormed out. He drove around the district, located his other hillbilly girlfriend, picked her up in the cop car, drove to Carondelet Park and had sex with her in the car.

Near relief at approximately 0630, Milton's hillbilly girlfriend from the apartment entered the Carondelet station house and asked to speak with Acting Sergeant Harry Freeman.

Harry knew her, and her family. "Give this to Milton," she said handing Harry the ring Milton had given to her. "I don't want anything to do with him anymore."

Harry Freeman took the ring from her and examined it. It was something that had come out of a Cracker Jack box. "You might as well throw this away little girl," Harry advised her. "It isn't worth anything, it's plastic."

The hillbilly girl stormed out of the station house. Harry Freeman tossed the ring into the trash. The event was another episode for Acting Sergeant Harry Freeman to add to the dossier of Patrolman Milton Brookins.

Patrolman Milton Brookins—compliments of the Mercantile Library

Patrolman Milton Brookins after his arrest by 7th district officers.

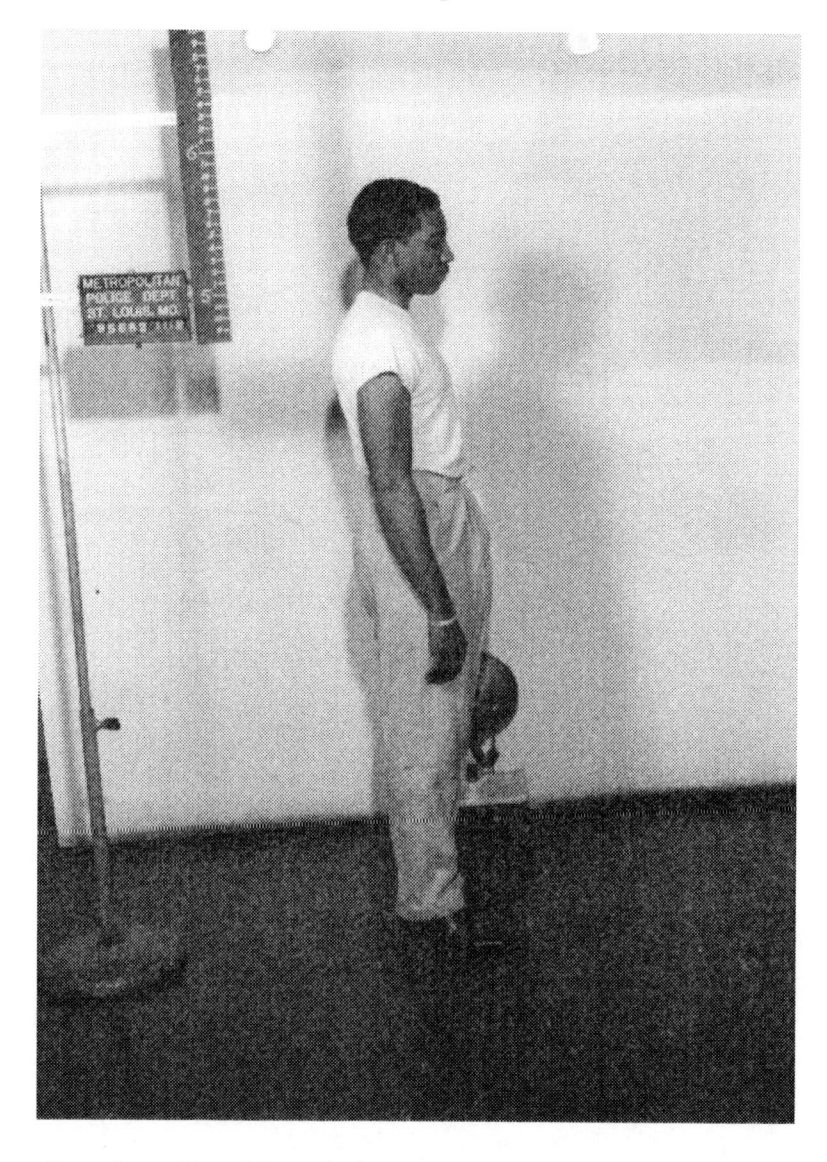

Patrolman Brookins—being booked at police headquarters.
Courtesy of Detective George Hotsenpiller

Tim Richards

Detective George Hotsenpiller.

Detective Bobby Matthews—with his prosthetic ear.
Courtesy of the Mercantile Library.

Retired Detective Sergeant Ron Adler.

Acting Sergeant Harry Freeman.

Killer cop--- Lieutenant Fred Grimes.
Compliments of the Mercantile Library

Lt. Colonel John Doherty
Courtesy of the Mercantile Library

Captain Barney Mundt.
Courtesy of the Mercantile Library

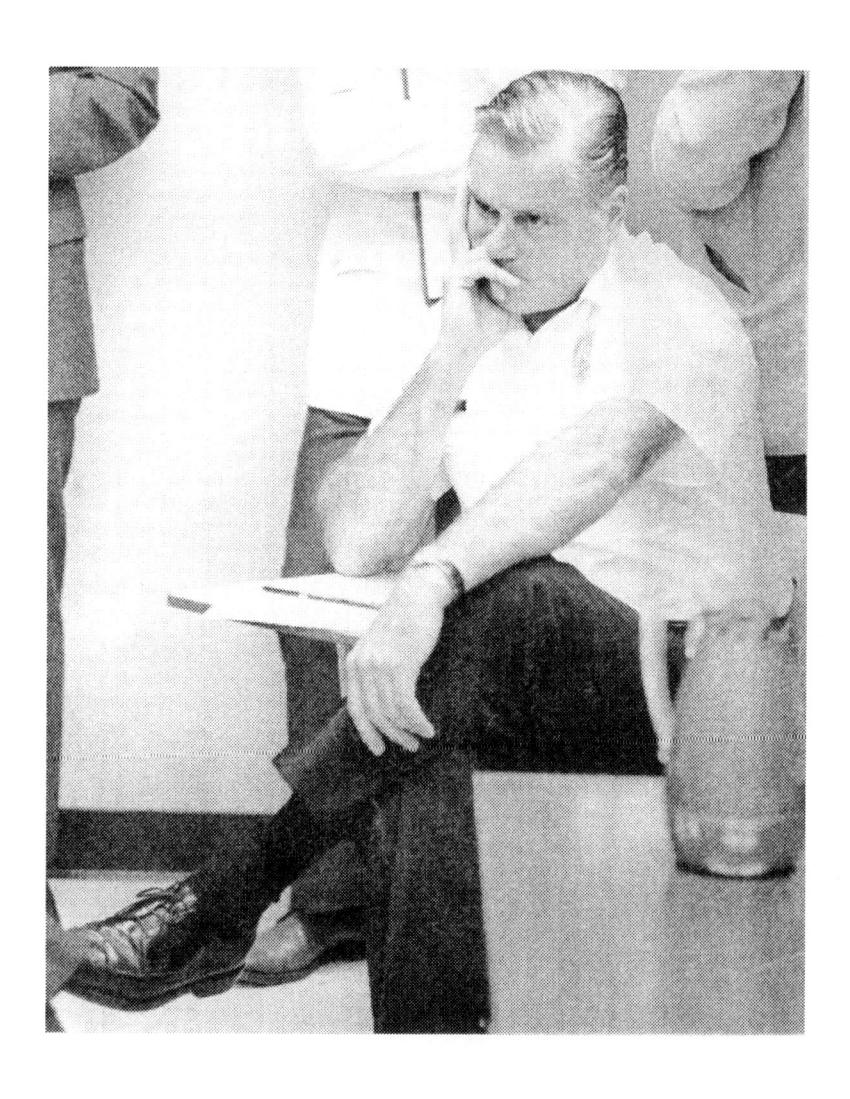

Captain Harry Lee, courtesy of the Mercantile Library.

Connie Rosenbaum---one of the many victims of Patrolman Milton Brookins. Courtesy of the Mercantile Library.

11

Detective Sergeant Chester Blancett was the type of supervisor who knew his men and knew their capabilities. He needed a detective Crew that would work tirelessly to catch the Phantom Rapist, but as in all endeavors, there must be motivation.

In the case of the Phantom Rapist, motivation was the hatred of a black man raping numerous white women and getting away with the crime.

In the eyes of some of the detectives this was a crime against nature. It was unspeakable, and thought upon as akin to child molestation.

Detectives George Hotsenpiller and Bobby Matthews were the detectives Sergeant Blancett had chosen to solve these heinous crimes. In his mind he figured they would have had the cases "cleaned up" by now. They had never let him down.

"You "fuckheads" been working on that damned Phantom Rapist case?" he asked.

"Yeah, boss," Bobby replied. "We're on it."

"I haven't seen any supplemental reports or memorandums referring to his capture or identity. The captain is going to be on my ass if something isn't done. You want me to take it away from you and give it to my number two crew?"

"We're on it, sarge," George replied.

"Get it done," he ordered them.

In those ancient times cops had two offices; the one at the district station, and a field office which was usually a tavern with friendly owners and a cute barmaid.

The Elephant Lounge on Pershing at DeBalivere was the "hang out" bar for George Hotsenpiller, Bobby Matthews, and scores of seventh district cops. George and Bobby were as close as brothers, both real country, real prejudiced, and damned smart.

The bar had a large plastic Elephant head nailed to the wall. Over indulgence at the bar was referred to as "going on safari." Being on safari meant shooting the elephant head.

The head was riddled with 38 caliber bullet holes. There were so many shots at the elephant that the owner continually had to move it from one wall to another while he patched up the holes.

George and Bobby discussed their strategy at the Elephant after the assignment of the Phantom Rapist case. "It's a fucking cop," Bobby Matthews began as they decided what their opening move was going to be. "I know it and you know it."

Bobby was the most vocal and flamboyant—George could control him when Bobby was sober, but when Bobby was drunk nobody could control him.

Part of their success in solving crimes was the interview. George would start interviewing victims, witnesses, and suspects with a country gentleman's tone. He would instill a feeling of trust and concern.

Victims and witnesses need to be led. George could and would accomplish this task. After there is trust, there is communication. Communication is the key to solving crime.

But George had to be the lead detective. Along with being flamboyant, Bobby Matthews was "scary" to all who viewed him.

He only had one ear. In days of old, cops could, and would, drink for free at a beer spigot at the Anheuser Busch Brewery. The only requirement was that the cop had to bring his own cup, mug, or glass. It was like a water spigot except fresh Budweiser would come from it instead of water.

It was placed there especially for off duty cops, and scores of city cops gathered there at the end of the afternoon watch to partake of the free brew.

As was usually the case, the cops got rowdy after several hours of free beer. There was a bathroom inside of the brewery that the cops had access to. They could walk inside of the giant brewery, relieve themselves in the restroom, and gawk at the operation as they returned to the free beer.

There was a one man lift inside, near the bathroom which went to the second floor. A cop advised Bobby Matthews that if he took the lift upward he could get a better view of the vats, and actually see the beer being brewed.

Bobby took the lift, watched the brewery in action, and then tried to take the lift back down to the ground floor. It was the kind of a lift that a person using it had to hang on with both hands, and place one foot on a step.

After several hours of free Budweiser, Bobby couldn't get the nomenclature of the lift in his brain. He hesitated, and his foot slipped, which made him swing while holding on with both hands as the lift was moving down.

Something caught Bobby's right ear and tore it off. There was nothing left but an ear hole. Bobby let go as his ear was being ripped off of his head and landed with a thud on the ground below.

Several drunk cops heard him fall and ran to his limp drunk body lying on the concrete slab below the lift. It was not a pretty sight seeing a uniformed cop, drunk with his ear torn off, blood spouting out of the side of his head.

Somebody got a towel and placed it on his head to stop the bleeding. Another cop got Bobby a fresh Budweiser to help with the pain. Bobby slugged it down. "Anybody see my fucking ear?" Bobby asked.

The cops searched frantically for the ear, but their search

was to no avail. "We've got to keep this quiet," a cop said. "If the brewery or the chief's office gets word of this we'll never get free beer again."

"We've got to devise a plan, make-up a story," another cop said while Bobby held the towel to his head and searched for his errant ear.

"Help me find my fucking ear," Bobby said. "If we can find it I can get it sewed back on." The bleeding was getting worse and the towel wasn't stopping the gushing flow of blood. Bobby's entire shirt was soaked, and he was starting to get weak from loss of blood, and excess of alcohol.

"I'm out of here," several cop buddies said as they walked away from the scene leaving Bobby to fend for himself.

"They'll fire you for drinking in uniform," one cop said. After hearing that remark most of the drunk cops fled the scene.

A security guard, who was at one time a city cop, drove onto the scene of the missing ear caper. "Hey guys, what's up?" he began.

The guard viewed Bobby with his head gushing, got on the radio and requested brewery emergency first aid staff to respond to the scene. Bobby was down and out by the time the brewery first responders arrived. They subsequently conveyed him to Firmin DesLoge Hospital.

An emergency room doctor sewed up the gaping hole in Bobby's head, and sent him home. The next day Bobby called in sick. Word of cop's bad behavior travels fast in the city P.D. It didn't take long before the chief's office and the inspector's office got word of the brewery event.

A team of inspectors responded to Bobby's door, knocked on it and were allowed to enter by Bobby's wife. Bobby was lying on the couch as they moved into his living room. His head was wrapped in a turban.

They demanded he tell them what happened. Even off duty, the City of St. Louis owns the cop's ass. Bobby told them what had transpired the night before, that it was a stupid accident, and that he had not been drinking.

The inspectors believed part of his statement. He was allowed to stay on sick leave until he was healed. The department was going to fire him, "conduct unbecoming a police officer"---a catch-all charge for wayward cops.

But the brewery intervened. Big business and state government controls the St. Louis Metropolitan Police Department. In the city, the brewery is the biggest business there is. Besides, the commanders, Chief on down the totem pole, desire free beer from the brewery. They do what big business tells them to do.

The brewery knew that if Bobby Matthews got fired from his job for drinking free beer at the brewery he would get a lawyer and sue the brewery for his injury. He would get millions from the brewery.

So Bobby was spared, and he made new friends at the brewery. One of his new friends got him transferred to the "Wild West" seventh district detective bureau. All was well in the continuing dilemma of cops and crooks. Now he was teamed up with his best buddy, Detective George Hotsenpiller.

George had to keep a close reign on Bobby. When George was "smoothing" a victim, witness or potential suspect, he had to keep Bobby from showing the right side of his head. Bobby's missing ear broke the focus of the person being interviewed. It had happened dozens of times. George would have to begin the mesmerism process all over again.

Bobby was given a prosthetic ear by the medical division, but he didn't care for it, and it turned green around the edges, and emitted a foul odor. When George complained about the smell, Bobby would remove it and place it in his pocket.

We've got to start interviewing these damned victims," Bobby exclaimed. "There's got to be something they can tell us that they haven't told those other dicks."

"We could start there," George agreed. "Which one do you want to start with?"

"The ones in the seventh have been interviewed by every damned cop in the district. They've looked at dozens of mug shots. I think the water is muddied up for them. They're used up."

George had a stack of reports in front of him. He picked one out and held it up for Bobby to peruse. "How about this little gal at the Chase Park Plaza, the receptionist? We could go there and interview her while she's at work, maybe get a free meal from the Chase. They give free food to the bloody ninth district cops, and besides this little gal is real cute. I saw her one day when I was at the Chase hustling a free meal."

"Great idea," Bobby said. They left the Elephant advising the barmaid that they would be right back and headed west toward Kingshighway and Lindell.

They parked illegally and entered the hotel. It was grand, something they did not have in the "Wild West" seventh. They felt out of place in their cheap suits and dingy white shirts. They had the odor of a rotting building, musty and stale with a hint of moth balls thrown in for flavor. But it wasn't their fault. Any human who ventured into the nasty seventh district station came out with its odor.

They approached the desk, "Pardon me ma'am," George began while showing her his badge, "are you the person who had the encounter with the rapist in her apartment on West Pine?" They knew it was her, but it was the only "lead in" George could think of at the time. The cute young girl had them both mesmerized.

She looked at them with distrust----Bobby kept the right side of his head turned away from her which made him look sideways at her, like a parrot that's preparing to either bite the voyeur in the face, or snatch a morsel of food from them.

"Yes," she finally said.

"We'd like to talk to you for a couple of minutes if you have a break coming, "George said. "We'll be sitting right over here in the corner."

"Okay," she replied. George and Bobby walked to the south side of the lobby and sat in modern overstuffed chairs waiting for her.

"This fucking ninth district has got everything," Bobby said as they waited. "And it's all for free for district cops." George did not comment.

After approximately ten minutes the cute rape victim walked to them, and sat down across from them. "Can we talk here?" She asked.

"Yes," George replied. "George handed her a composite picture of the rapist. "Does this do anything for you," he asked.

The victim studied the picture. "It looks like the same man," she said, "but I can't be sure."

"Is there anything you can tell us that maybe you remembered after your initial interview with the ninth district detectives?" George asked.

"She thought for an instant, "No, actually I've been trying to forget the whole thing, but I will know that man if I ever see him again. I will never forget his voice and his walk. He was cocky and arrogant, and it showed in his walk."

Bobby intervened. "Is there anything unusual about him?"

She hesitated, "No, just a black man, light complexion,

muscular, not fat, solid type of a guy."

George rubbed his forehead---he knew it was coming--- "Was he hung?" Bobby asked. "Did he have a big dong?"

"About average for a black man," the victim replied without hesitation.

"Okay, ma'am," George said while standing. We'll be in touch when we find this guy."

Bobby turned so that the right side of his face was visible to her. She gasped, then looked away. "Any chance we could get a comp'd lunch?" Bobby asked.

"Oh, yes," the cute girl replied, "Follow me."

They followed her into the hotel to a fine restaurant off of the lobby. She approached the maître de, "Seat these gentlemen and bring the tab to me."

"Yes, ma'am," he replied. "Right this way, gentlemen." They followed him to a rear table, sat and waited for the server.

The room was like a fancy restaurant in Atlanta or Savannah. It was tropical, wrought iron tables with glass table tops, and bamboo high backed chairs. There were large whicker ceiling fans slowly moving throughout the room. The diners were dressed casually, but expensively.

They studied the menu and were approached by the waiter. "May I get you gentlemen a drink from our bar?" he said.

Bobby started to order. "No, I mean we'll have Cokes," George said. "In fact, we can order lunch now if that's okay."

"Yes," the waiter replied.

"I'll have the strip steak, medium rare, French fries, and a salad with ranch dressing."

"I'll have it the same way," Bobby replied.

"Thank you gentlemen," the waiter replied as he walked away from them.

Bobby was brooding. George could read him well and he took note of a mood change. "That victim was a real cutie wasn't she?" George stated.

"Yeah, she was cute, but I wouldn't do her."

"What?" George exclaimed. "You'd do her in a heartbeat."

"Nope, I swear to you I wouldn't," Bobby continued. "Did you hear her response when I asked her about the size of the Phantom's dong?"

"Yeah, I heard it," George replied. "It sounded okay to me."

"Not to me," Bobby continued. "She said his dick was about normal for a black guy. In my mind that means she knows about black guys' dicks. She's probably seen many in her short life. That means she fucks NIG-row's. I would never go into some bitch who's had a black dick in her. My daddy would come back from the grave and cut my balls off."

"You really think she knows about black dick?" George asked.

"Yep!" Bobby replied. "In fact, I'm wondering if she really is a victim of a rape. She may have flirted with that damn Phantom and enticed him to look her up. If she knows about black dick, then she's capable of enticing the Phantom. I'm crossing her off of my list of girls I want to fuck."

"Okay, I understand," George said. They both laughed.

"What would your daddy do if he found out you fucked a gal who had had black dick in her?" Bobby asked.

"Come back from the grave and cut my balls off," George replied.

Diners were glancing at them as they loudly laughed, noticing Bobby's head hole, and their cheap smelly clothing. Their conversation was heard by several tables of diners.

A middle aged man with his wife began clearing his throat and staring at them. Bobby made certain they saw the right side of his face. "Fuck them," he said to George.

George studied his old friend Bobby. Nobody knew Bobby Matthews like his partner and friend, George Hotsenpiller. "Did you go on safari last night?" George quietly asked.

"Yep," Bobby replied with a smile.

"Did you shoot the elephant?" George asked.

"Right between the eyes, five times," Bobby replied.

They ate their meal and slowly exited the dining room. The cute receptionist waved to them as they walked out of the lobby. They waved back.

They entered the junky detective car and drove around the Central West End. They were on Maryland Plaza, a trendy shopping area for the elite of St. Louis. Beautiful and classy women were slowly making their way from shop to shop, spending big money for things they did not need.

They drove by the rape locations, from Forest Park to West Pine, to Euclid, and then to McPherson. They were like blood hounds searching for a scent, looking for anything out of the ordinary. The scent was not there.

"We need a break," George said. "We can interview these fucking victims until the cows come home, but we ain't gonna accomplish anything. We need a fucking break."

"The trail is cold," Bobby agreed. "Maybe something will come up."

"It's about relief time at the district stations," George said. "We could hang out at one of the north districts and see if we see any Negro cops who look like the Phantom."

"Yeah, that sounds like a winner. Which one do you want to go to?"

"Well," George said in deep thought, "The bloody ninth has already eyeballed most of the Negro cops in their district. We've taken a close look at most the blacks in our district. Maybe we should branch out to the sixth, and the eighth, and then work our way south to the first, second, and third."

"Yeah, man, I like it," Bobby said. "But, I don't think there are any black cops in the first, or second."

"Yep," George replied. "I think you are right on that one."

They drove north to the sixth district station which sat across from the Calvary Cemetery. The cemetery was historic, having Civil War Generals and beer tycoons honored with grand granite mausoleums. They parked in the parking lot and strolled inside.

They stood at the desk and watched as the shift changing cops made relief. There were about fifty cops coming and going, maybe six of them were black, and none of them fit the description of the Phantom.

"Fuck this," Bobby said. "Let's go to the Elephant. This shit ain't working."

They drove back to the Elephant Lounge and hung out at a back table. "We're going to have to come up with something," George began. "The sarge is going to be pissed if we don't start showing some kind of an investigation in this damned case."

"Something will pop, George, just you wait. It always does for us."

12

Patrolman Milton Brookins was on another long stretch of off days, and he was intent on pursuing his hobby, the raping and robbing of young white women.

At 2:10 P.M. on March 3rd at # three South Euclid, Milton lightly tapped on the door of a twenty year old nursing student. She opened the door, Milton said, "Do you know Kathleen Harper?"

"No," the victim replied. Milton pulled his snub nosed revolver and pointed it at her face. He pushed the door completely open and forced himself into the apartment. The victim backed away as Milton closed and locked the door.

"Don't scream, all I want is money," Milton calmly advised her. He pushed her into a bedroom, took a pair of black gloves from his pocket and put them on, then observed the victim's wallet lying on a table in the bedroom. He grabbed the wallet and took $16.00, all the money the victim had, then tossed the wallet onto the floor.

Milton stuck the money and the revolver into his trousers pocket and pulled out a knife. He opened it and showed it to her. "Don't look at me, take off all of your clothes, I'm going to tie you up so you can't follow me."

The victim removed her clothing except for her bra, and panties. Milton cut the cord from a clock in the bedroom and tied her hands behind her back, laid her onto the bed and covered her face. He tied her ankles with the cord from a lamp in the room.

"I'm going to leave for a few minutes," Milton said as he left the bedroom. He turned on the record player. Milton entered the room nude. He removed her panties and the cord around her ankles, and raped her. The victim began crying. "Why you crying, baby, you been fucked before," Milton whispered to her.

Milton did not ejaculate. He climbed off of her and dressed. "Where's your typewriter?"

"Living room," victim replied. Milton went to the living room and typed a note to the ninth district cops:

Hello Stupid coppers:

Victim number 55
The Phantom Fucker strikes again.
More will follow.

Signed,

The Phantom Fucker

Milton returned to the bedroom, "I typed a note for the cops. Make sure they get it." Milton went into the bathroom and turned on the water in the sink, returned to the bedroom and said, "I'll be back before I leave. Milton left the apartment. Victim went into the kitchen, got a knife from the drawer and cut herself loose.

Patrolman Tom Daley in charge of car Ida nine responded to the scene. Tom was a good guy and a steady cop. He did things correctly, and he was well liked by his peers and his supervisors. He treated the victim with respect and called a paddy wagon for her to be conveyed to City Hospital # one.

He called for the finger print man to respond, and the department photographer. He seized her panties, left the scene, and resumed the patrol of his area. No prints available due to contamination.

Cordell Brown, Chief Criminalist for the St. Louis Metropolitan Police Department, responded to the scene at # three South Euclid. He seized a pillow case, a dress, numerous lengths of electrical wire, and the note typed by Milton Brookins.

Milton was getting wilder, and he was infatuated with the women at the Ambassador Hotel, 108 N. Kingshighway. On March 19th he forced the lock on an apartment while the thirty six year old resident was preparing to get into the shower.

She thought she heard a noise, so she wrapped herself in a towel and went to investigate. Milton was waiting for her. He knocked her to the floor and began choking her. He choked her until she passed out. Milton cut a cord from a lamp and beat her with it on her back and sides while she was unconscious.

Milton then shaved her pubic area with a straight razor, scraping and cutting it as he shaved it. He raped her on the living room floor while she was unconscious.

She regained consciousness one time while he was raping her. Milton said, "I told you I wanted you, and I got you." The victim lost consciousness again. When she regained consciousness, she was lying on the living room floor. She noticed that she had been shaved, and that she was beaten, scraped and cut. She called the police.

Patrolman Oliver Wood in George nine received the call. He was shocked by the victim's account of what had happened to her. The bloody ninth district cops knew that eventually the Phantom Rapist was going to become more violent as his rapes continued.

Ollie Wood wanted to take the victim to the hospital, but she refused. She had a friend who was a physician and he had a practice nearby. Dr. J.M. Ornstein responded to the scene and treated the victim. Ollie Wood seized her panties and left the scene.

Detectives George Hotsenpiller and Bobby Matthews heard about the new rape in the bloody ninth district. They decided to go to her apartment and interview her.

They tapped on the door and eventually were allowed entry. The victim could not give them anything substantial since she was knocked unconscious.

"Tell us about your pussy being shaved," Bobby blurted out. George placed his hands over his eyes, Bobby had done it again.

"I mean, he cut your private parts while he shaved you, right?"

"Sir," the victim began. "I have a fiancé, and he isn't taking well the fact that his loving girlfriend has been raped by a black animal. We were supposed to be married next week. He has called it off. If I conceived during the rape by that monster then I, all by myself, will have to make arrangements to have an illegal abortion. Things aren't good for me right now, and I wish you guys would please leave my apartment."

The detectives stood and walked out.

Milton was getting reckless. He randomly chose an apartment he hadn't done surveillance on. On March 24th at 11:40 A.M. Milton was parked Taylor and Laclede---near the West Pine, Kingshighway, and Forest Park corridor that he frequented for rapes.

He observed a twenty one year old victim walking toward an apartment building at # fifteen South Taylor. Milton got out of the Phantom rental and followed her. She walked to the building, and Milton continued to follow her to her apartment on the second floor. She entered her apartment and locked the door.

Milton did his routine, knocked on the door and said, "I have mail for you." Victim opened the door and Milton was pointing his pistol at her. "I'm looking for Dennis Hagen," Milton said.

"There is nobody here by that name," she replied.

Milton forced his way into the apartment, "Don't look at me or you'll get hurt," he said to her. "Is there anybody else in the apartment?"

"Yes," the victim replied. "My fiancé and his friend are in the bedroom."

The fiancé and his friend came into the foyer and observed Milton with the pistol pointing at the victim. "Oh, I'm sorry," Milton said, "I was looking for Dennis Hagen." He stuck the revolver into his pocket, turned and walked away. The victim and the witnesses observed him enter the Phantom Rental and drive away.

Patrolman Robert Frye received the assignment. He took their information, got a detailed description of Milton and his Phantom rental, and had the radio dispatcher broadcast the vehicle description over the air.

Milton had avoided arrest again. He was angry with himself for botching the rape of a cute young white girl. He decided to go back to his old standby area, the one with the Washington University students, the "Wild West" seventh.

He had seen a cute white girl walking along Waterman at about Kingshighway previously while he was prowling in the Phantom Rental. She was just perfect for him, petite, young, and vulnerable.

He followed the potential victim to her apartment building at 5092 Waterman, exited the Phantom Rental and followed her to her apartment. He decided to wait for a better day to ravish her. There were residents in the hallway. They would be witnesses when the police did a canvas. Today was the day for the girl at 5092 Waterman.

It was just three short hours, and four city blocks away after the botched attempt on South Taylor. Milton parked

Phantom Rapist

the Phantom Rental on Kingshighway at 2:30 P.M.

At approximately 2:45 P.M. Milton entered the building on Waterman, walked up the stairway to the third floor and tapped on the door of apartment three-A.

The twenty one year old student, and part time key punch operator, dressed in a nightgown, opened the door, and observed Milton. "I have a package for Mrs. Peterson," Milton stated.

"There's nobody here by that name," the victim replied.

"I deliver packages here all of the time for her at this apartment," Milton said.

"Well, there was a girl by the name of Coleman who lived here before me."

"Yeah, that's it," Milton said. "It must be her sister. Do me a favor." Milton pulled his revolver and pointed it at her. "I don't want to hurt you, I just want your money."

Milton grabbed the victim's nightgown, forced his way into the apartment, closed the door, and turned her around so that he was behind her. He pushed her into the kitchen. The victim's black purse was lying on the counter. Milton took it and removed $2.00 from it, then tossed it on the floor.

"You have more money than that, don't you?" Milton asked.

"In the bedroom in a metal box there's some more," the victim replied. "Please take it and leave."

Milton pushed her into the bedroom, removed $10.00 from the metal box, and stuffed it in his trousers pocket. "Take it off," Milton said as he tugged on her nightgown. The victim removed her nightgown. Milton removed her panties and bra. "Lay on the bed."

The victim complied.

"I'm going to fuck you," Milton said as he pulled his trousers off. "It'll feel good because I'm so big."

Milton raped her for a few minutes, then got off of her.

"Were you ever curious of how it tasted?" He placed his penis in her mouth and ordered to suck on it while he watched the sex act in the bedroom mirror. Milton then raped her again, ejaculated and climbed off of her. He dressed.

"I'm expecting some company," the victim said hoping to frighten Milton into leaving. "It's my girlfriend, she's coming over."

"If she gets here before I leave, I'll fuck her, too," Milton advised.

Milton placed a pair of black leather gloves on and searched the apartment. He found a silver dollar in a drawer, and pocketed it. The victim again dressed in her nightgown. Milton forced her into the kitchen and made her sit in a kitchen chair. "Don't look at me," he said to her.

Milton moved around the apartment while the victim sat in the kitchen. He examined her stereo record player, "I guess you don't want me to take this, do you?" he asked.

He returned to the kitchen, "Do you have anything I can use to tie you up?" The victim did not answer him.

Milton cut the cord of a mixer, forced the victim back into the bedroom and tied her wrists. "I have to tie you up because one time I didn't tie a girl that I fucked, and twenty minutes later I was in jail. I did seven years for that one. I'll die before I go back to jail." He tied her wrists with the electric cord, and tied her ankles with a dog leash that was lying on the floor.

"Don't move," Milton ordered her. "I'll let you know when I'm leaving." Milton then left the apartment carrying her portable television, and an F.M. radio. He also stole her driver's license and her keys.

Victim heard her front door close and then heard a car door, and a car start up at the rear of her apartment. It took her an hour to free herself. She called the police.

Patrolman Roy Stern got the assignment. He recorded her story, seized her panties, then conveyed her to Missouri Pacific Hospital on South Grand in his scout car. It had become a discretionary decision on behalf of the investigating police officer as to what hospital the victim wished to be taken to.

Detectives Rodger Kohler and Warren Williams of the seventh district bureau responded to Harold's Pawn Shop at 4901 Delmar. They advised the owner Harold Feingberg, that they were looking for a stolen General Electric portable television with tin foil on the rabbit ears, and a Longines-Symphonete World Traveler AM-FM radio.

The pawn broker retrieved the stolen items from his inventory and showed them to the detectives. The victim positively identified the stolen items.

Harold Feingberg stated he could not remember what the person looked like that pawned the items, but he had a name of William Harris, with an address of 4353 Washington.

The detectives drove to the address on Washington. It was a vacant lot.

Detectives Hotsenpiller and Mathews interviewed the victim. Before Bobby could ask her about the size of the rapist's penis, the victim made the following statement: "I've been around a lot of St. Louis cops. They have a way about them, a presence. They talk and conduct themselves differently than normal people. The guy who raped me was a St. Louis cop. If the police department doesn't realize it, then it is a stupid organization. I don't wish to talk to you guys anymore. Please leave."

Bobby and George exited the apartment.

At 2:30 P.M. on the same day, March 24th, Milton drove the Phantom Rental to 4411 Forest Park. He had been on surveillance there several times, watching a twenty three year old medical student. He had followed her to apartment, two south. Today was her day to experience the slave stud, Patrolman Milton Brookins.

Milton parked the Phantom Rental on North Taylor and walked to the apartment building. He took the stairs up to floor 2, and knocked on apartment two south.

The victim looked out to the hallway and observed Milton standing at her doorway holding some papers, and magazines in his hand. "What do you want?" she asked without opening the door.

"I'm from the apartment manager and I have to check some things in your apartment," Milton replied. The victim opened the door, Milton pistol paralyzed her, shoved his way inside, closed the door and locked it and said, "Don't make any noise, all I want is money."

"I only have 15 cents," the victim replied.

Milton pushed her further back into the apartment, "Are you alone?"

"Yes," the victim replied.

Milton placed his revolver to the victims head and forced her to go with him to every room in the apartment. He turned off the lights inside of the apartment. Milton noticed a bed in the dining room. "Who lives here with you?"

"I have a lady roommate," she replied.

"When will she be home?" Milton asked.

"About 5:00 this evening," the victim replied.

Milton forced her into the bedroom. "Get undressed and get on that bed," he ordered with the revolver pointing at her face. He placed the revolver in his pocket and pulled out a knife.

"What are you going to do to me?" the victim asked.

"Shut the fuck up and do as you're told and you won't get hurt," Milton said. He covered her face with her skirt, removed her panties, removed his trousers and attempted to insert his penis into her vagina. "Help me get it in," he ordered.

The victim complied.

Milton raped the victim. During the rape the victim stated, "You are hurting me." Milton stopped.

"Get some damned Vaseline," Milton ordered her. She went into the bathroom with Milton following her, got a jar of Vaseline from the cabinet and took it back into the bedroom.

"Rub it on my dick, and then rub some on your cunt," he ordered her.

The victim complied.

"I'm on my period," the victim said.

"Oh, fuck," Milton replied, "But I'll fuck you anyway. Help me get this dick into your cunt."

The victim complied.

Milton raped her for approximately forty minutes. He forced her to get into several positions. She did not know if he ejaculated.

He climbed off of her, dressed and asked her for some typing paper. Just lie on the bed. I'm going to write the police a letter." He went to a desk in the bedroom, inserted the typing paper and wrote the letter:

Hello Police:

It's me again your neighborhood rapist, otherwise known to you as the Phantom Fucker.

This woman is my 2nd one today. I fucked Dawn on Waterman in those new apartments about 1 block west of Kingshighway on the south side of the street.

She did not have a typewriter. I also fucked a woman last week in a hotel, but I did not have time to find out her name

because she wanted to fight, and I had my hands full.
  She was # 56, Dawn was # 57, and this lady is # 58. Excuse my poor typing. It's hard to do with gloves on.
  I will fuck more women soon.

Phantom Fucker

  Milton returned to the bedroom and tied the victim's wrists and ankles with some cord that he found in the apartment. "Don't try to get loose," he ordered her.
  Milton left the bedroom. The victim heard him rummaging through the apartment, and then heard water running in the bathroom.
  Milton returned to the bedroom and took the typewriter off of the desk. He walked out with it. "Don't try to get loose until I'm gone," he again ordered the victim.
  She heard her front door close and she started using her teeth to get free from the bindings on her wrists. She cut the cord from her ankles with a pair of scissors.
  She tried to use the telephone but it was tampered with and would not work. The mouthpiece had been removed. She went to a neighbor to call the police.
  After returning, she looked around her apartment. Milton had stolen her Singer sewing machine, her portable RCA stereo, and her portable typewriter.
  Patrolman John McCahan, and Gerald Walters, in charge of car G-9 received the assignment.
  Patrolman McCahan interviewed the victim. Patrolman Walters started knocking on doors looking for a witness He found an 11 year old girl. She advised him that she had seen a black man exiting the apartment carrying a TV, a radio, and a sewing machine. She held the front door open for him because his arms were full of the items.
  The patrolmen seized the victim's panties, and conveyed

her to City Hospital # one.

Two eighth district detectives, Russell Smith and William Cox, assisted by Robert Downey and Gene Oitker, received information from a reliable informant that a subject known to the informant may be implicated in the rapes and robberies occurring in the West End and the Central West End of the city.

Armed with this information, the detectives went to the suspect's home and took him into custody. He was conveyed to the eighth district bureau and interrogated by the detectives.

He was advised that he had been implicated as a possible suspect in the Phantom Rapist case, and advised that he would be taken to police headquarters and placed in a department show-up.

The suspect requested that he be able to contact his lawyer. He was granted the request. He contacted Attorney Curtis Crawford.

After consulting with his attorney, he advised the detectives that he would not make any statements, and that he would cooperate with them.

The rape victims from 5092 Waterman, # three South Euclid, and 4627 McPherson were contacted and agreed to meet the detectives at police headquarters.

The suspect was placed in a show-up with several individuals, and was viewed by the victims individually. They could not identify him as the person who had raped and robbed them.

The suspect was conveyed back to his residence, and advised that no further investigation of him would be conducted by this department based on the informant's information.

13

Detectives George Hotsenpiller and Bobby Matthews were sitting in the seventhdistrict detective bureau going over rape reports. It was April, and the Phantom Rapist had been raping and terrorizing single white women in the central corridor for almost three months.

"The ninth district locked up a couple of rapists, Bobby commented. "They even got a positive I.D. and a warrant issued on one of them. But the Phantom Rapist continued to rape these goofy door-opening-women. They eventually let the guy go. He'd spent about two weeks in the workhouse awaiting trial. Assistant Circuit Attorney Melroy B. Hutnick made a rational decision that the guy they had locked up was the wrong guy."

"You mean the victim recanted her positive identification?" George Hotsenpiller asked.

"Yeah, that's what I meant," Bobby replied. "You know," Bobby continued, "It never ceases to amaze me as to why these stupid victims open their damned doors. For at least two months the newspapers, and the local television stations have been warning the public about the Phantom Rapist. They go into detail on how this guy knocks on doors of young white ladies, pistol paralyzes them, forces his way in and rapes them. And it's all done in the West End and the Central West End. But the rapes keep occurring, the victims still open their doors, and the Phantom keeps eluding capture. It blows my mind."

"It's blowing the mind of the captain, the major and the chief, too," Detective Sergeant Blancett commented. "They continue to ask me if we are making any headway. I told them I've got my best crew on it. They are waiting for some results. So am I. You geniuses have any fresh ideas?"

"We're working on it, sarge," George replied. "We just

need one little break and we'll get this guy. Nothing has popped, yet, but it will. You'll see, he'll make a mistake and we'll be on him like stink on shit."

Sergeant Blancett did not reply. He dug his face into supplemental reports as if he were a college student studying for an exam. George came up with a plan: he and Bobby would walk around the alleys in the West End during the daylight hours.

If they saw someone looking suspicious they'd stop them and see if they had a gun on them. If the guy acted scared, or told them a lie, they would bring him into the 7seventh bureau and interrogate him with phone books.

George ran the plan by Sergeant Blancett. They all liked it. George and Bobby began their trek through the West End alley ways.

George particularly liked this plan. It got him out of a detective car with Bobby Matthews. Bobby had a hygiene problem; he didn't bathe very often, and he hardly ever changed his socks.

Any detective who ever rode with him complained about the stench. It was said that Bobby's socks were crusty and so was he.

As luck would have it, the detectives observed an alley creature climbing through a gangway window into a ground floor apartment. They waited for him to come back out, guns drawn.

The burglar climbed out and came face to face with Bobby Matthews, standing with his gun drawn. Bobby didn't plan it that way---he had gotten nosey and was trying to peer into the open window.

He turned his back on the window and was mouthing words to George, making signs with his hands and arms while the burglar was silently climbing backwards through the open window. George observed the burglar's buttocks, and right leg of the big window climber coming through, and he tried to warn Bobby, but it was too late, they were standing near each other, both with drawn guns.

The burglar fired, and missed. Bobby fired and missed. Bullets were ricocheting off of the granite stone foundations. Bobby tried to run toward the street, but slipped and fell, injuring his foot and ankle. His crusty prosthetic ear came off and was rolling down the gangway after him.

The burglar ran toward the alley----George was waiting for him. "Drop it or you're dead," George calmly said. The burglar gave up. They conveyed him to the seventh district bureau for torture. Bobby went to the hospital for treatment.

"It was a good arrest," Sergeant Blancett told them--- "But this guy wasn't the Phantom Rapist, and the ultra-liberal victim doesn't wish to assist the state in the prosecution of this felon. The Circuit Attorney doesn't want to pursue the matter because the victim won't cooperate, so in actuality, all that was accomplished was that Bobby Matthews fell and broke his sock."

Milton had been out of commission for about a month, working the day watch and laying low. He had made up with his apartment sharing girlfriend, and was living there part time. He spent more time there than he did with his wife.

He was no longer mesmerized with the hip and cool Laclede Town. The white women there unknowingly teased him. They were beyond his reach, too close to home for his special treatment for forced brutal rape. Their presence at the pool in bikinis tortured him.

He still had the hillbilly girls in the first district to unleash his sexual desires upon, but as was always the case, he demanded more.

The thrill of the hunt intrigued him, the call of his

hunting grounds called him, and the fear he instilled in his victims charged him with a surge of energy and excitement.

The winter was about over for St. Louis. It was April 22, and Milton was again on the prowl, but he was about to make a costly mistake. All criminals do. Cops who turn into criminals are the worst for making stupid mistakes and getting caught.

They feel successful in their criminal crusades after a series of scores, whether it be stealing or raping. If they get away with the crime more than once, they get cocky and feel they are untouchable. Cops trick themselves into thinking they are super criminals. They think they know the system and that's what gets them caught.

Milton had been stalking a young woman who lived in an apartment at 6149 Waterman. He had followed the Washington University student home from the campus approximately a month earlier.

She lived in apartment # eleven, and she was the perfect victim for him, twenty years old, petite and cute.

Milton arrived at the apartment building about fifteen minutes earlier than when he had previously observed the potential victim. He knew her schedule. Had she had a dental appointment, or needed to study at the school, or had decided to go shopping, Milton would have gotten bored and left the building. But the victim was right on-time.

Milton was standing behind a staircase on the 3rd floor approximately fifteen feet from her apartment door. The victim took the stairway up to the third floor, but failed to see Milton. She went to her apartment, unlocked the door and walked inside.

She observed Milton running at her with a gun in his hand. He grabbed her by the back of the neck and pushed her into the apartment. He did his usual, "Don't scream and you won't get hurt, I only want your money,"

He continued to hold her by the back of her neck and he pushed her around the apartment in front of him, searching every room, and turning off the lights. He engaged her in conversation, asking her name, and her husband's name.

He found her purse, dumped it on the dining room table and rifled the contents. He pocketed her driver's license, a Phillips 66 credit card, her apartment keys, her car keys, and $5.00 in cash.

"I've been doing this for a long time," he advised her. "I can't leave by the front door." Milton tried to open the kitchen door leading to a fire escape but couldn't get the door open.

He pushed her into the bedroom, replaced the gun with a knife and put it to her face. "You won't get cut if you do what I tell you to do." Milton removed his leather gloves.

"Take off your damned clothes and get on the bed," Milton ordered her.

The victim complied.

Milton removed his trousers and got on top of her. "Have you ever fucked a Negro?" he asked.

"No," the victim replied.

Milton licked the victim's vagina for a couple of minutes, then inserted his penis into her and raped her. He did not ejaculate. He climbed off of her and licked her vagina again for approximately five minutes, then raped her again. He ejaculated, climbed off of her and licked her vagina again.

Milton got up and pulled on his trousers, "Get up and get dressed," he ordered her. He tied her wrists and ankles with an extension cord, and then left through the front door with the television under his arm.

The victim chewed at the cord until she freed herself. She called the police.

Patrolman Stan Dylewski in charge of car Henry seven received the assignment. He took her information, seized her panties and the bed sheets, and conveyed her to the hospital.

14

The victim of the April 22nd rape was furious at herself for allowing Milton to enter her apartment and victimize her. She was not only a victim of rape, her husband was having a difficult time coming to grips with the fact that his beautiful, young, and intelligent wife had been violated by a Negro.

She pondered the rape, and wondered how she was targeted by The Phantom. She went over in her mind her daily routine; school, and home is all she did.

She came to the conclusion that the rapist must have seen and targeted her at the Washington University Campus. She was correct in her assumption. Being a student in a world class university one would think that the assumer would know what transpires when one assumes. Assumptions make asses of us all.

On April 29th on a bright spring St. Louis morning, the victim observed a man trimming the grass on the campus. His name was Isom Combs Jr., a twenty year old refugee from the Great State of Mississippi who came to St. Louis to help his parents raise their eleven children.

The Combs family lived at 6439 Myrtle in Wellston. Isom played guitar in the church choir, he was hired as a laborer by Washington University, and he gushed out his happiness to anyone who would listen. He loved his job, and he loved being in St. Louis.

Coming from Mississippi, St. Louis held a new found freedom he had been promised by pastors, school teachers and black activists. Any job in St. Louis would be better than any job a black man in Mississippi would have.

As he worked on the grass edges, he observed a white female student approach his supervisor and engage him in conversation. They kept looking at him, and the student pointed at him several times.

It wasn't long before the University City Police came and arrested Isom Combs. He was quickly transferred to the St. Louis Police holdover, and held for forcible rape and sodomy. He was interrogated by detectives, and asked if he was the Phantom Rapist.

Isom had read about the rapist committing his crimes in and around the Washington University Campus in the local newspapers. He denied the accusation. He asked for a lie detector test to prove his innocence. The request was ignored.

His dad came to visit him and told him he would try to get him an attorney. Criminal defense attorneys require thousands of dollars up front to defend someone against a type one felony charge. The Combs family were poor southern blacks trying to survive up north. He was represented by a public defender.

He wanted to make bond, but again, bonds took cash up front. In the State of Missouri, a professional bondsman must be used in felony cases. The bondsman requires a non-refundable ten percent fee up front. If the bond is set by a judge at $20,000, the person making the bond for the prisoner must come up with $2,000.

Poor folks languish in jail, getting beaten, sexually assaulted, and starved awaiting trial, even though they are innocent until proven guilty.

Isom was officially booked on the charges, and was placed in a lineup. The victim of the April 22 rape positively identified him as the person who accosted her in her apartment on Waterman.

The Circuit Attorney's office issued charges against Isom Combs Jr. and he was transferred to the St. Louis City Jail. He was placed in a six man cell that was housing eight prisoners.

The St. Louis City Jail was notorious for its treatment of prisoners. It was 100 years old, and had the look and smell of a dungeon.

Ison Combs Jr. had an alibi. He was working for the University at the time of the rape. The St. Louis Police Department contacted his supervisor and asked him about the alibi.

The grounds crew supervisor stated that he was on the work schedule but he was not physically seen by the supervisor at the time of the rape.

Isom was beaten daily by the other prisoners. His first beating was in the "day room", a place where the prisoners can watch television.

A prisoner asked him why he was in jail. "They said I raped some white girl," Isom replied.

"We don't like rapists in here," the prisoner said, and several prisoners beat Isom unconscious.

The jail guards did nothing to stop the beatings. One of their specialties was placing young white men prisoners into a cell with several black prisoners. They watch as the white prisoner is beaten, sexually assaulted, and forced into performing sex acts for the other prisoners. It is the most evil of the evil of inhumane acts perpetrated by jail guards.

The white prisoner, in those days, was "on his own". So were young, country-blacks. There were no white guards in the City Jail at that time. The pay was $5,000 a year, about the same as a patrolman on the police department.

Isom advised that about every other day when he was in the cell with the other prisoners he would be beaten. He was afraid to get up and move around the cell, so he sat in a corner near his bunk. One of the prisoners would come to him and beat him with their fists and feet, leaving him unconscious.

He would awake bloodied and battered and another

inmate would beat him unconscious. At one point he was beaten twice in one day in his cell. At night a guard came into the cell, removed him from the other prisoners, took him into a hallway and beat him unconscious.

During the evening meal prisoners would take food from his tray, leaving him with just enough food to stay alive. It was the same men who regularly beat him.

Isom said he never tried to defend himself. There were too many men beating him. He tried to cover up but they still knocked him unconscious.

He was told by one of his attackers that the guard who beat him was named Colin Tripp. Later, after Isom was released, an investigation revealed that there had never been a guard named Colin Tripp working at the city jail.

Isom suffered from a broken nose, a punctured ear drum, a brain concussion, and broken teeth. He was never taken to a hospital by the city jail staff.

During his painful incarceration Isom thought back to his youth in Mississippi. He was never beaten there, just discriminated against and mentally abused by the "white devil."

The southern blacks warned him against going to St. Louis. "They'll jail you up there and you'll never get out," they would tell him. "All blacks look alike to those "Yankee white devils" in St. Louis."

Isom didn't believe them. Anywhere was better than Mississippi. Now he was second guessing his decision on coming to St. Louis. He prayed while his fellow inmates beat him. Every punch on his face and body was followed by intense prayer. It was all he knew, he came from a faith seeking, God fearing family. His prayers were eventually answered.

Detective George Hotsenpiller received a phone call from Bobby Matthews in the early morning hours, "Come into work now, the night crew have got a guy in custody who fits the description of the Phantom Rapist. They're torturing him right now, trying for a confession. If you're not here, the other crew will get full credit for the arrest. Get your ass in here."

George climbed out of bed and high-tailed it to the bureau, located on the third floor of the haunted house police station.

Bobby met George on the first floor, "There's a problem with this guy."

"What kind of a problem?" George asked.

"The night crew worked on him a little too hard, and they killed him."

"How the fuck are they going to explain that?" George asked.

"We've got a plan," Bobby replied while wiping perspiration from his forehead. "We're going to throw his body off of the balcony adjacent to the bureau offices. He'll land on the front steps, and that will explain his injuries. We're going to say he tried to escape while being questioned about the rapes. He ran and jumped off of the balcony."

"You think that will work?" George exclaimed.

"It's our only option, the guy's dead as a door nail, heart attack or something."

"I'm not going up there," George stated.

"You don't have to. We want you to stand here near the steps to block foot traffic. We don't want any coppers hurt by a flying dead body. Just make sure nobody uses this door for a while until we toss him out. He weighs a ton, it's going to take three of us to hoist him over the railing."

"Okay," George replied. "I'll block traffic." George waited for 20 minutes and there was no flying body. Bobby came back downstairs.

"False alarm, that fucker came back to life. He's being released right now; they're pushing him out the back door of the station, into the alley. Hopefully he'll make it a couple of blocks away before he dies. He wasn't the Phantom Rapist anyway, but you and I both know, he's good for some felony---he's victimized somebody in his life, probably worse than what we did to him. It's righteous!"

George shook his head, "I guess so, Bobby."

On May 10th, the victim from the April 22nd rape at 6149 Waterman contacted Detectives Hotsenpiller and Matthews. She had received an invoice stating that her credit card had been used at Doyles Phillips 66 Service Station at 4225 Lindell on April 23rd the day after her rape, and robbery.

The detectives went to 6149 Waterman and further interviewed the victim. She showed them the credit card invoice. It was for an oil change, and a change of snow tires. There was an Illinois license plate number on the bill, 642-022.

"I'm having a difficult time letting go of this episode in my life," the victim stated. "You know, that animal acted like he was doing me a favor by raping me. Can't you guys catch him before he strikes again? I don't wish this on anybody."

"We're trying, ma'am," George replied.

The detectives returned to the station and contacted the Illinois Department of Revenue. The license was current, not reported stolen, and was issued to a person in Wood River, Illinois.

"Sarge, we're going to Wood River, Illinois," George Hotsenpiller advised the detective sergeant. "This may be the clue we've been waiting for."

"Yeah, yeah," Sergeant Blancett replied. "There's been an arrest in this case. It's probably over. This guy in the city jail is going to eat every one of these damned rapes. You guys are a little late on this one."

"I don't think the mope in the city jail is the Phantom Rapist," George replied. "Bobby Matthews doesn't think so either. Just because one victim identified the guy doesn't make him the Phantom."

"Alright. Stay in touch with me, and notify the command post," the sarge replied.

And besides, sarge," Bobby Matthews said, "I heard they've got a street over there in Wood River named "Whitelaw." I've got to see that one. There's supposed to be free of any Nig-rows. They aren't allowed to be in the town after dark. You ever heard that?"

The sarge sneered, waved them off and continued reading reports.

The detectives drove to Wood River, Illinois and were met by Sergeant Ralph Skinner. He conveyed them to the address of the issue of the Illinois license plate.

The gentleman owning the vehicle advised them that his car was being driven by his daughter and that she lived and worked in the St. Louis area. His daughter was a nurse at Barnes Hospital, and she lived near the hospital.

The investigation in Wood River was complete. "Is it true y'all don't have any Nig-rows in this town, and that you've got a street named Whitelaw?" Bobby Matthews asked the Wood River sergeant.

"It's true," he replied. "I'll show you the street." He drove them down Whitelaw, pointed out the street sign and then gave them a tour of the city. "Refineries," he said pointing. They smell, and the air is polluted but it's a good paycheck for the folks who can get hired to work there. Swimming pool," he again said while pointing. "Largest public pool in the area, bigger than some lakes. Refineries built it for the residents." He took them back to their car.

"Is it true that Nig-rows have to be out of town by nightfall?" Bobby asked.

"That's an old law," the sergeant continued. "Back in the 1920's a Negro shot and killed the chief of police in Wood River. The law was enacted at that time, but it's not enforced."

The detectives entered their car and headed back to St. Louis. They went to the station, and advised the sarge of their findings, then responded to the address of the car owner's daughter.

The detectives, along with the owner's daughter inspected the vehicle, and found that the front license plate was missing. It had been stolen. In Missouri, at that time, only one license plate was issued by the state. Milton stole the Illinois license plate, stuck it on the rear of the phantom rental, and used it undetected.

The detectives drove to 4255 Lindell, Doyle's Phillip's 66 Service Station, and interviewed Ed Doyle, owner of the business. Ed Doyle was friendly with the command personnel of the police department. He worked on their cars, and their relatives cars, gratis.

The station was a hangout for ninth district cops, local celebrities, successful businessmen, and high ranking cops from headquarters. Ed Doyle got many patrolmen promoted to sergeant, or moved into a prestigious detective job.

Ed Doyle immediately advised them of his status within the hierarchy of the St. Louis Metropolitan Police Department and that he was able to get cops promoted, transferred or disciplined.

It was the pecking order of business owners and police department politicians. The participants were proud of their clout within the department. Political clout was a game and a hobby. They bragged to anyone who would listen. Street cops knew who the influential businessmen were. If given the chance, they would cultivate them, befriend them and eventually use them for political favors.

The cop seeking political assistance was part actor, part politician and part cop. There was always a sad story involved; the cop would advise the businessman that one of his children is ill and he needed to make more money. Or that he needed a downtown detective job that supplied a take-home car.

The cop mentally would pen a script, one that would peak the interest of the businessman and motivate him to pick up the telephone and make the call to the chief's office. George and Bobby knew the drill and were aware of the procedure. They acted impressed.

Ed Doyle was shown the invoice from the Phillips 66 credit card stolen from the victim of the May 22nd rape on Waterman. He shared it with his mechanics, one of whom was an organized crime associate and who also had the ability to pick up the telephone and get a cop promoted. After some deliberation they agreed that they remembered the car and the driver.

They were shown photos of suspected rapists in the case. They were not able to make any identification from the photos, but they gave a good description of the vehicle: a 1969 dark blue and black Chevrolet. The driver had forged the victim's husband's name.

They dragged themselves back to the station without any viable information. It was nearing relief time for them, they called it a day and headed for the Elephant Lounge.

They were drinking at the bar, drowning their troubles with discounted booze, and interacting with the other cops hanging-out, doing the same thing.

Bobby Mathews was conversing with Patrolman Gary Tucker about the Phantom case. "I know it's a city cop," Bobby said. "We're just having a hard time finding out who this guy is. We need a break."

"You know," Gary Tucker began, "I stopped a guy in the 6100 block of Pershing one night back in late April. I asked him what he was doing in the area, and he told me he was a city cop. He showed me his badge, and I thought it was kind of weird because his badge was in his pocket, loose. It wasn't in a badge holder. I've got his badge number written down in my notebook."

Patrolman Tucker pulled out his notebook and rummaged through it. Cops are trained to write everything down in their notebooks. When a notebook is filled with clues, the cop tosses it in a drawer or at the bottom of his locker. The notebooks are dated when they are opened, and the date they are full. "Here it is, this is the guy's badge number."

Bobby took the notebook and stared at the number. He wrote the clue down in his notebook---"Me and George will check this out tomorrow morning."

Detective George Hotsenpiller was at work early at the raggedy seventh district detective bureau. It was always that way when there's a fresh clue in a case that had been haunting him.

He was on the phone with the command post. He had given the desk officer the badge number that Patrolman Gary Tucker had provided Bobby Matthews the night before, and he was waiting for the command post officer's response.

"Milton Brookins," George exclaimed. "I never heard of him. Is he a Negro?"

"Yep," the command post officer replied.

"Where is he assigned?" George asked.

"First district," the command post officer replied.

"You sure?" George replied. "I didn't know there were any Negro cops in the first district."

"He's the only one," the command post officer replied.

"Okay, thanks!" George hung up the phone and waited for Bobby Matthews to wander in. It was just 07:30, and Bobby wasn't due in until 08:00 or so. George's next step in the investigation would be to call the personnel division and obtain a photo of Patrolman Milton Brookins. The personnel division didn't open for business until 0900. He went over rape reports and drank coffee.

15

Milton could have laid low and let Isom Combs Jr. take the fall for most of his rapes, but he didn't. Milton was proud of his accomplishments. He was The Phantom Rapist, and he didn't want to have anybody take that prestige away from him.

On May 14, Milton was on surveillance in the 4400 Block of Westminster, in the fashionable Central West End. He had seen a young white girl living in the apartment building at 4411 Westminster several days earlier and had followed her to her apartment on the 2nd floor, rear.

Milton entered the building and waited in the shadows for the victim to open her door. It didn't take long, and the victim opened her apartment door to leave for the day.

Milton grabbed her, stuck his revolver in her face and forced her back into the apartment. He did his routine on her—forced her back into the bedroom and ordered her to remove her clothing.

The victim removed her clothing while Milton ransacked the apartment, apparently looking for money. He took her Nebraska driver's license and $6.00 in cash.

Milton beat her, ravaged her, scratched her with his fingernails, raped her, then tied her ankles and wrists with nylon stockings. He blindfolded her and gagged her, and left her on the bed, unconscious.

Milton was preparing to leave the apartment when someone tried to enter the apartment with a key. Milton had the night chain on the door, and when it opened partially, Milton slammed it shut.

The person trying to gain entry to the apartment was the victim's roommate, and another girlfriend. She thought the victim was playing a game with her, so she stated, "Come on, open the door, stop playing games."

Milton opened the door and stuck his revolver in their faces. "Get your asses in here and you won't get hurt," Milton growled at them." Both girls entered the apartment. Milton slapped them around, kicked them, made them cower in a corner and robbed them of their Nebraska driver's license; they had no money.

"Get into the bathroom," he ordered. They complied. "Stay in here for five minutes after I leave, and I won't come back and hurt you." Milton slammed the door.

The girls in the bathroom waited for approximately five minutes, walked into the apartment living room, and heard the victim struggling in the bedroom, gagged, tied, and naked. They untied her and contacted the police.

Patrolmen Dennis Townsend and James Brawley, in charge of car Lincoln nine responded to the scene. The victim was hysterical and could not give much of a detailed statement, but she advised the officers that she had been raped.

She was conveyed to Firmin Des Loge Hospital in a paddy wagon, accompanied by Patrolman Brawley. Milton had apparently become overly zealous with this victim. She was admitted, and was diagnosed as having numerous scratches, abrasions, of her throat, neck, and abdomen, as well as a torn vagina. Patrolman Townsend seized her panties.

It was apparent that Isom Combs Jr. was not the Phantom Rapist, the descriptive term given to Milton by the press. But he still languished in the city jail, and was continually beaten by guards and inmates.

Detectives George Hotsenpiller and Bobby Matthews wondered how long it would be before Milton killed one of his victims. The Phantom Rapist was morphing into the Phantom murderer.

Detective Hotsenpiller was on the telephone with the personnel division. "I need a photo of a first district patrolman," he advised the clerk.

"I'll have to have the director call you back," he replied. George hung up and waited.

In five minutes the phone rang and George answered it. "We can't give you a photo of an active police officer," the personnel director advised. It's against the rules and regulations of the police department. We gave the ninth district bureau a photo, and the police officer had a lawyer call us and ask us what authority we had to give his photo out for an investigation. After some deliberation, the police officer agreed not to sue the city and the Board of Police Commissioners."

"Okay, thanks," George replied and hung up. He dialed the 1st district desk, "Can you tell me what hours Patrolman Milton Brookins is working today?"

"He's off today and tomorrow, "the desk officer said and slammed the phone.

"What's up?" Detective Sergeant Chester Blancett asked.

"Patrolman Gary Tucker stopped a guy back in April in the 6100 block of Pershing. The guy is a Negro city copper, and showed Tucker his badge. Tucker wrote it down, and after a couple of beers last night, he showed Bobby Matthews the badge number. I called the command post this morning. The Negro cop's name is Milton Brookins, and he's assigned to the 1st district. I contacted personnel and requested a photo of him. The director advised me that it was against police department rules and regulations to give photos out to other cops."

"Carondelet District?" Sergeant Blancett exclaimed. "I

didn't know there were any Negro cops in that district."

"Apparently he's the only one," George replied. "I called the district and Patrolman Brookins is off for today and tomorrow."

"Call the record room and find out where he lives," Sergeant Blancett said. "We can run surveillance on his house, take a picture of him, and add it to our list of suspects' mug shots."

"Okay, Sarge," George replied. George dialed the record room and requested an address on Milton Brookins.

"2912 Red Maple Walk, in Laclede Town," the clerk advised him.

"Okay, thanks," George replied, preparing to hang up the telephone.

"Wow, that's weird," the clerk continued. "This guy's got a local identification number. He's been arrested, do you want his number?"

"He's been arrested?" George asked.

"Yeah, C.C.W. gun. Warrants refused. He's got a photo. You want it?"

"Yeah, I'll be right down."

Bobby Matthews and Sergeant Blancett were standing at George's desk. George glanced up at them. "This cop's been arrested, they've got an L.B. photo of him."

Sergeant Blancett waited for his "crack" crew to figure out what their next step would be. "Me and Bobby will go down and get the photo, Sarge. We'll take it to the Phillips 66 station on Lindell and see if the guy Ed Doyle can I.D. him."

"Okay," the Sarge mumbled.

Patrolman Ron Adler and Sam Lackland had been reading the supplemental reports written by Detectives George Hotsenpiller and Bobby Matthews, and were armed with the vehicle description of the car serviced at Doyles Phillip's 66 Service Station on Lindell with the credit card stolen during the rape on Waterman. In their minds, the guy driving the car had to be the Phantom Rapist, or knew who the Phantom Rapist was.

They were working the day watch, riding, conversing, and watching for the suspect car. They saw it east bound on the Forest Park Expressway, and followed it.

Milton observed them following him and ducked into a car wash at 4600 Forest Park, in the bloody ninth district. Ron Adler and Sam Lackland followed Milton into the car wash, and engaged Milton in conversation.

"City copper," Milton said as he was getting out of his car. He held up his badge for Ron and Sammy to see. He left the car door open as he smiled and talked with the two cops.

Ron Adler noticed the service sticker from Doyle's Phillips 66 Service Station in the door-jam of the Phantom rental. They took note of the Illinois license plate on the rear of the vehicle.

After inspecting Milton's credentials, they allowed him to leave. Milton put the car in the car wash line, went inside to pay for his wash and watched the patrolmen drive back to the seventh district.

Detectives George Hotsenpiller and Bobby Matthews, armed with a photo of Milton Brookins, drove directly to Doyles Phillips 66 Service Station on Lindell.

They placed Milton's photo in the batch of other rapist photos and showed all of them to Ed Doyle. Ed picked out Milton's photo as the guy who used the stolen credit card to him for work done on the Phantom Rental.

The detectives showed the batch of photos to the mechanics in the garage who worked on the Phantom

Rental. They all chose Milton's photo.

George and Bobby headed back to the seventh district station. When they arrived, George telephoned the first district and asked for a supervisor, he got Acting Sergeant Harry Freeman. He asked Harry to check on the dates of Milton Brookins day's off related to the dates of the rapes in West End and Central West End. George didn't relate the rape investigation to Acting Sergeant Harry Freeman. As far as Harry Freeman was concerned, Detective George Hotsenpiller was just another nosey city cop checking on an associate.

Milton was either off on recreation, sick leave, or accrued court time.

"He's got an apartment with a district hillbilly white girl at 6329 Alaska," Harry advised. "He's there more than he is at his home on Red Maple Walk."

"Thanks," George replied.

Detective Sergeant Blancett went directly to Captain Barney Mundt's office and advised him of the detective's findings.

Patrolmen Ron Adler and Sam Lackland responded to the seventh district detective bureau with their information about stopping Milton Brookins in the suspect vehicle serviced at the Phillips 66 Station on Lindell.

"There's a Negro cop driving that vehicle," Ron Adler advised.

"Yeah, we know," George replied. "His name's Milton Brookins, here's his photo." George held the photo up for them to look at.

Sergeant Blancett came out of the captain's office. "George, you and Bobby go down to the 1st district, to 6329 Alaska and do a surveillance on Brookins' apartment. If the suspect vehicle is there just covertly sit on it and wait for me to contact you."

"Yes, sir," George replied. He and Bobby Matthews headed out the door.

"Ron," Sergeant Blancett continued. "You and Sammy also head down to the first, but just to back up George and Bobby. Stay out of sight. I don't want this rapist cop to see any of you guys until we're placing him in handcuffs. Got it?"

"Yes, sir," Ron replied. He and Sam exited the office. Sergeant Blancett exited the office headed for police headquarters.

George and Bobby rolled onto the scene down in the Carondelet neighborhood. The Phantom Rental was parked at the curb in front of 6329 Alaska. They drove by and located a covert parking place out of sight of the apartment building where they could conduct surveillance on the car and the building.

George had the radio dispatcher contact Sergeant Blancett and advise him that the suspect vehicle was "on the scene."

Detectives Hotsenpiller, Matthews, and Patrolmen Adler and Lackland watched, and waited for instructions from Detective Sergeant Blancett.

After approximately 1 hour, Detective Sergeant Blancett rolled onto the scene in the backseat of a brand new, black Buick staff car. The Buick was being driven by Lieutenant Colonel Eugene Camp, Commander of the Bureau of Field Operations. He was soon to be the new Chief of Police.

Riding shotgun was Lieutenant Colonel Robert Matteson, the Inspector of Police. They met up with the officers, and as they were devising a plan to arrest Patrolman Brookins, Milton exited the apartment house and entered his Phantom Rental.

"Take him down," Lieutenant Colonel Camp ordered. George and Bobby drove to Milton as he started to drive away with a red light on their dash---they blocked Milton in, and the command Buick pulled up alongside of Milton.

Milton got out, "Police officer," he said with his badge held in the air."

Patrolman Ron Adler and Sammy Lackland then pulled in front of Milton's Phantom rental, exited their car and walked back to the other officers.

Milton was still holding his badge up in the air with his right hand. "You're under arrest," George advised Milton.

"For what?" Milton asked.

"Fraudulent Use of a Credit Device, Improper State Vehicle License, and Stealing over $50.00 (auto)," George advised Milton.

Ron Adler grabbed Milton's badge out of his hand and pocketed it. Milton glared at Ron Adler—"You can't imagine how hard I worked to get that badge," Milton stated. Ron ignored his statement.

The following day, May 21st, a show-up was conducted at police headquarters. Milton was placed in the show-up with five other men with the same coloring, build, and age.

Eighteen rape victims responded to the show-up. Also in attendance was Assistant Circuit Attorney Melroy B. Hutnick, three attorneys from the public defender's office, and a high ranking black police department commander. Detectives Hotsenpiller and Bobby Matthews coordinated the show-up.

Each of the victims was brought into the show-up room separately. The men in the show-up were ordered to make statements that Milton had made during his rapes and robberies. When Milton was ordered to speak, he would jut his jaw out and talk in a high pitch, trying to disguise his face and voice. Some of the victims became physically ill, some became hysterical---all were angry, humiliated, and disgusted.

Seven of the rape victims identified Milton Brookins as the man who had raped and robbed them. Milton was held over pending warrant application. Assistant Circuit Attorney Melroy B. Hutnick issued rape and robbery charges against Milton Brookins. He was held, pending a bond hearing.

Milton's parents came back into his life. They hired him a good attorney, Dan Reardon. He tried to make bond. His bond, for some reason, was fixed on the charges of two cases of rape, and one charge of auto theft.

Earlier, Judge Richard Brown of the Court of Criminal Correction advised Milton Brookins' lawyer that he would fix bail at $25,000 each on the rape charges, and $1000 on the auto theft charge.

Dan Reardon objected to that amount of money set for the bail. Judge Brown stated that the normal amount of bond for a rape charge is $5,000 per offense, because it is considered an aggravated case. Judge Brown advised Dan Reardon that he could go to another judge if he wanted to try and get a lesser amount for Milton Brookins bond.

Dan Reardon went to Judge Casey Walsh with an application for bail. Dan Reardon convinced Judge Walsh that if Milton Brookins bond was set at $51,000, the court was, in effect, denying Milton Brookins his constitutional right to get out on bond.

Judge Walsh set the bond at $12,000. His parents used their home on St. Louis Avenue for security for the bond. Milton was free on the bond.

Milton's dad, the same dad who told him "go out and populate the world," gave him a car to drive.

On the night of the bond for Milton Brookins, Patrolman Ron Adler and his wife were celebrating Ron's chance at greatness within the police department.

Ron was going gangbusters on Colonel John Doherty's country cabin on Dardenne Creek. Now Ron had gained notoriety with another high ranking cop, Lieutenant Colonel Eugene Camp, the next Chief of Police.

Ron and his wife were dancing and dining at the Tick Tock Club on DeBallivere in the West End. It was a grand night. Ron and his wife had just finished dancing and were returning to their table. Ron got bumped into, hard. He almost fell down. He looked at the person who bumped him, it was Milton Brookins. Milton apparently had Ron and his wife under surveillance. He was stalking them.

Milton looked Ron in the eyes, said "Oh, excuse me," smiled, and walked off of the dance floor. Ron watched as Milton exited the club.

On June 25th, Detective Bobby Matthews received a letter in the mail. The anonymous letter threatened Bobby Matthews if he testified against Milton Brookins. It was post marked in East St. Louis, Illinois, and stated that "death would come to anybody who testified against this fine man."

The letter also mentioned George Hotsenpiller, Ron Adler, Sam Lackland, Colonel Eugene Camp, Colonel Robert Matteson, and a few other officers who worked the case.

Brookins' neighbors in Laclede Town were skeptical of his guilt. They were in disbelief. A "Brookins defense fund" was opened at the Gateway National Bank. A spokesman for the defense fund stated, "The group and fund was started because we feel that Milton Brookins is being persecuted, and has already been found guilty because he is a black man accused of raping many beautiful white women."

He said further, "We are not saying whether he is guilty or innocent, because that is for the courts to decide. The same type of front page guilty treatment was given to Isom Combs Jr., and now they say he is innocent. This could happen to Milton Brookins."

The spokesperson for the members of the defense fund stated that they did not select the Gateway National Bank because it is conveniently open on Saturdays, "we chose it because it is operated by black people who will be sympathetic to our cause and work with us."

One female resident of Laclede Town stated, "If he wanted to have sex with white women, he could have done that right here. He didn't have to go outside of our community."

While Milton Brookins was out and about on a discount bail, stalking the police officers who investigated his rapes, writing threatening letters, and driving around the streets of St. Louis in his dad's car, Isom Combs Jr., the young man mistakenly identified by the Washington University student as the person who raped her, was still incarcerated in the St. Louis City Jail. He was still being beaten and starved.

Shortly after the show-up at police headquarters and after Milton Brookins was positively identified as the Phantom Rapist, the victim from the 6100 block of Waterman went to the St. Louis Circuit Attorney's office.

She spoke with Assistant Circuit Attorney James A. Roche Jr., and advised him that she had mistakenly identified Isom Combs Jr. as her assailant. She stated that she had positively identified Patrolman Milton Brookins Jr. as the man who had raped her. She requested that Isom Combs Jr. be released.

Isom Combs Jr's. lawyer, Barrister Dobberstein, also spoke with Mr. Roche concerning the release of Isom Combs Jr.

Mr. Roche took their requests for the release of Isom Combs Jr. under advisement. It took an additional twelve days for Isom Combs to be released.

When questioned by the press as to why Isom Combs wasn't released immediately, Mr. Roche stated that the circuit attorney's office wanted to question her further regarding her identification of Brookins and Isom Combs.

There was the Memorial Day Holiday involved, and the victim was out of town. The circuit attorney's office didn't want to release Isom Combs Jr. and then have the victim return to their offices and state that she had changed her mind.

After the eventual release of Isom Combs Jr., he returned to work at Washington University. But he was too sick to work. The brain concussion and the punctured eardrum kept him from doing anything but staying in his family's home in Wellston.

Isom was treated at the Washington University medical center and told to remain at home until he was healed. He advised close friends that he was in fear of going outside.

An investigation was launched by the press of the City of St. Louis. Arthur J. Kennedy, city welfare director, admitted that such violence is a common occurrence at the city jail. "Anything that can happen in the streets can happen in the jail," Kennedy said.

Kennedy was interviewed while he was attending a legislative barbeque in the State Capitol of Jefferson City, Missouri. "Without more guards at the jail, inmates will continue to be beaten, robbed, and sexually molested by other prisoners."

The white community was incensed that a black city cop had raped and ravaged dozens of young, bright, educated, and refined white women, but they weren't surprised. St. Louis city cops were noted for their strangeness. It's a trait they learn through osmosis.

The black community was enraged that a young,

innocent, church going, laboring, never before arrested black man could have been thrown into the city jail, beaten, starved, and tortured for a crime he did not commit. All told, Isom Combs Jr. spent 35 days in the dungeon city jail.

A grand jury was called to investigate the Combs incarceration case. Circuit Judge Casey Walsh charged the jury: "You are instructed to inquire into the matter and report to this court."

Circuit Attorney James Corcoran prided himself on the transparency he instilled in his office. He met with newspaper reporters and editors on a weekly basis for a "discussion breakfast" at Miss Hullings every Monday morning. Whatever the press desired from his office it was given to them. At times he would give the press complete investigative and court proceeding reports. He was taken aback with the Isom Combs Jr. incident.

Alderman C.B. Broussard submitted a resolution to the Board of Alderman asking for the City Counselor to compensate Isom Combs Jr. for his loss of pay during his incarceration. He also requested that the city police and the Federal Bureau of Investigation investigate the report that Isom Combs Jr. had been beaten during his incarceration.

A group calling itself Concerned Black Women, headed by Miss Joyce Ladner, met with Judge Casey Walsh. "We are enraged over the travesty of justice which Combs received at the hands of the St. Louis Metropolitan Police Department."

Judge Casey assured them the Grand Jury would get to the bottom of the problem and fix it. The group then met with Circuit Attorney James Corcoran and issued the same complaints to him. They advised him that Combs told the police that he was not the Phantom Rapist.

Mr. Corcoran stated that the accusation was incorrect---Combs was asked two times for a statement, but he refused to give one.

The ladies group then advised Mr. Corcoran that Combs had an alibi, that he was working during the rape, but the police arrested him anyway without checking his alibi.

"Incorrect, again," Mr. Corcoran replied. "The police checked with Mr. Combs' supervisor. He was listed to work that day, but the supervisor did not physically see him during the time of the rape."

The ladies group met with Curtis Brostron, Chief of Police. He advised them he would meet with the Board of Police Commissioners and report the results to the women later.

During the Grand Jury investigation, Combs was summoned and given a request to point out the men who beat him while he was incarcerated. They had been transferred to the City Workhouse awaiting trial.

Arrested and charged with the Combs beating were: Donald Swink, twenty, who was in the city jail awaiting trial for the Assault with the intent to ravish a fifteen year old; girl, William Riley, twenty four, being held for stealing; Carl Terry, twenty five, awaiting trial for three counts of murder; and Larry Wayne, eighteen, who was facing first degree murder in the shooting death of a Lincoln University student.

It was a contest between the black community and the white community over who was violated worse, the victims of Milton Brookins vicious and perverted rapes of white women. Or Isom Combs Jr., the victim of being mistakenly incarcerated, beaten and starved.

The blacks had the Department of Justice working in their favor. Isom Combs constitutional rights had been violated, not only during his arrest, but during his incarceration, and the failure of the system to release him after Milton Brookins had been arrested for the same charge.

The white community had the criminal justice system working for them. They were foolish to think that the system would bring justice, or even solitude to the victims of Milton Brookins' brutal attacks. There is no justice, there is no peace, for anyone who places their trust in the criminal justice system.

The only thing the white community had going for them was the fact that they were white in a white dominated environment. They, as a politically controlling race, felt that was enough. It wasn't, and it isn't.

The blacks were and are organized. The whites are just white. The worm has turned for both races. Now the blacks are the politically controlling race in most cities in the United States of America, coddled by the federal government, and acutely aware of their constitutional rights.

Whites are still non-organized, tax-paying workers. Most of them don't know or care about their constitutional rights. They hire lawyers to protect their rights, instead of relying on the feds.

16

Milton Brookins was down, but not out. The grand jury indicted him on only two of the rapes he had committed. Two out of fifty is not bad odds in the criminal justice system.

His lawyer, Dan Reardon, had tried rape cases before. The jurors have difficulty identifying with the victim. There is always a feeling of distrust between them. The defendant is a St. Louis Police Officer, a family man, a person of integrity. There is a chance that Milton could "beat the rap" on the rape charges. The victims would not look good on the stand. Dan Reardon would make certain of that.

Then there's the Phantom Rental. Brookins could take the stand and possibly explain why he did not return the rental. He could even say that he was not the person who rented the vehicle. The clerk at the rental agency would not be able to identify Milton. It had been too long since the transaction had taken place.

Then there is the testimony of the rapes. Milton would take the stand. He was a great liar; all cops are, it is basic survival instinct for people who put their lives on the line on a daily basis.

Then there is the Isom Combs Jr. incident, the positive identification of him as the Phantom Rapist, and the taking into custody of another St. Louis Police Officer, Myron Johnson.

Dan Reardon could show that the cops in St. Louis were grasping at straws in a feeble attempt to clean up the rapes, and with their effort they were arresting and trying to railroad anybody they could get their hands on.

The prosecution would try to grill Milton, but he'd be coached by Dan Reardon. Milton would deny being the person responsible for the two little rapes of these college coeds. The burden of proof is on the state. Milton would have to be proven guilty without a reasonable doubt. Can a jury in the City of St. Louis do that? Milton and Dan Reardon were gambling that they could not.

The prosecution would, at some point in the trial, ask Milton Brookins if he was indeed the Phantom Rapist. He would say, "No."

Dan Reardon would solidify his client's alibi by having Milton's wife, or maybe even a neighbor, take the stand and testify that Milton was at home during these alleged rapes. Milton would have his day in court, and there was a good possibility that he would come out a winner.

If he did win, he would sue the police department for back wages, and eventually get his job back. He would be a victorious criminal, still on the job as a St. Louis City cop. He could chase white women in the district he was assigned, and forget about his previous obsession with raping young white women.

In Milton's mind, he did nothing wrong. He was doing the women a favor by raping them. In his mind he was giving them the sex they desired, but could not get from their white boyfriends or husbands. It is what he had been taught; black men are superior to white men, sexually and physically. As his aunt Bessie said of Milton---"He's a sick little boy."

Milton was still prowling around the Central West End. He had given up on the West End, primarily because of Detectives George Hotsenpiller, Bobby Mathews, Ron Adler, and Sam Lackland.

These cops would know him on sight, and would pull him over, search his vehicle, and arrest him for the slightest traffic violation.

Before Milton was arrested as the Phantom Rapist, he

had seen a couple of potential victims on Euclid in the Central West End. Milton enjoyed raping and gawking on Euclid. The apartments he raped women in were "walk-ups" with street entrances. Most were above shops and restaurants.

These walk-ups had been used as apartments for decades, and the victims felt safe there. There was foot traffic on Euclid, and the Barnes Hospital and Jewish Hospital complexes were within walking distance.

The victims on Euclid felt safe because there is safety in numbers. It is herd mentality. It was the same feel on the Washington University campus. The students felt safe there, but Milton was mingling and watching, stalking and following, getting the information he needed to attack when the timing was best for him.

There were classy apartments on Buckingham Court, just off of Euclid, behind the Forest Park Hotel. They were expensive, and the most fashionable of any of the apartments in the CWE. Professional people and wealthy heirs lived there. It had a west coast vibe.

The Central West End was a combination of Greenwich Village in New York City, Haight Ashbury in San Francisco, and Sunset Boulevard in Los Angeles. It drew strange people to it, and these were strange times in the United States.

People were dropping out of society. The war in Viet Nam was killing the good, happy, healthy, hard-working young men of the country; the ones who would be productive citizens when they came back, if they came back.

The "drop-out" society became distrusting of the country's politicians. JFK had been gunned down in Dallas. Doctor Martin Luther King preached non-violence, but the blacks were killing each other in droves. He was eventually gunned down in Memphis several years later. LBJ was a president no one trusted, and the economy was in a downward spiral. People dropped out, and if they didn't have the moxie to go to San Francisco, Los Angeles, or Greenwich Village, they ended up in the Central West End.

Residents had abandoned many of the 1904 World's Fair mansions. They were stately, made of granite, with carriage houses and expansive grounds, large mature elm and pin oak trees, but most of them had at least two gigantic boilers to heat them. The boilers were powered by heating oil. There was an oil crisis, and the owners of these mansions usually ended up moving into just one or two rooms, or moving into their carriage house apartments.

In most cases, every room had a fireplace, and if the owner/resident was lucky, he would rent rooms out to the dropouts who walked the streets of the Central West End, looking for "weed" to purchase.

Milton had seen a beautiful "hippie" girl walking along Euclid on several occasions. She caught his eye because of her vulnerability and her youth. He tried to follow her to find out where she lived, but it didn't work out for him.

The "hippie" culture in the Central West End included the luxury of being independent. The Euclid Avenue dropouts didn't want assistance from the federal government. They didn't want food stamps, or free meals, they just wanted to fend for themselves in obscurity, almost as if they were invisible.

This beautiful "hippie" girl had a knack for design and art. She survived by advising wealthy clients how to decorate their mansions. She was as independent as a young person could get, she was only seventeen and on her own in the big-city.

If Milton could have followed her he would have seen that she lived above a carriage house at 4336 West Pine. The little apartment was barely livable, and if the city would have inspected it a permit for occupancy would not have been granted.

Being built over a garage it had little insulation----the floors were always freezing in the winter, and most of the time there was no hot water. But the place had character---it reeked of independence, and it was cheap, $100 a month.

Independence comes at a high price for a seventeen year old girl. She was an artist waiting to bud, and she had her own mind. She came from an artistic family—her dad was a musician, and she basically got along with him, but there were seven kids in one house, and she felt she was the one who should leave the nest and find herself. Laid back Webster Groves did not hold her interest.

In the state of Missouri, a person is defined as a juvenile if he or she is below the age of seventeen. Being in the Central West End, and living in a freezing carriage house was heaven to her. She was on her own and independent. It was all that mattered to her.

If she had to go anywhere over a mile, she hitchhiked. It was a reasonable way of transportation in those days. People hitchhiked all over the country. People bragged about hitchhiking to Los Angeles from St. Louis, with no money, and nothing but a Hershey bar in their pocket.

Milton had seen the "hippie" girl hitchhiking, and he was tempted to stop for her. He slowed and ogled her, and his perverted brain gave him images of her nude, blindfolded, gagged and hog tied on a bed somewhere, but he didn't pick her up.

Milton had a protocol: his modus operandi was to shock someone in their own domicile, a place where we all feel safe. The initial rush of fear instilled by a gun wielding black man while standing in one's own doorway was the key to his success as a serial rapist. Once the fear is instilled, the man with the gun remains in control of the situation until he decides to end it.

But he thought of the "hippie" girl frequently, and he wanted her badly, so badly that on this fine summer day he was prowling on Euclid looking for her. He was driving his dad's Oldsmobile 88, four door sedan. It wasn't a new car like the Phantom Rental, but Milton washed it every day so that it shined like a new vehicle.

It was what he was known for in the utopian society of Laclede Town----always washing his car. Milton was obsessed with cleanliness.

He had another potential Euclid Avenue victim that he had seen and was obsessing over. Her name was Connie Rosenbaum, and she was 180 degrees from the "hippie girl".

Connie was educated, refined, smart, and a professional person. She was a reporter for the liberal St. Louis Post Dispatch, and she was just twenty two years old---three years younger than Milton Brookins. Her dad was a famous neuro-surgeon at Barnes Hospital. She was everything Milton had wanted in a rape victim.

In Milton's mind, if he could just get Connie into a rape/sex situation, and give her slave stud satisfaction, she would be addicted to him, love him and be his sex slave. It worked for Milton, and he was going to give it a try.

Milton had previously observed Connie walking on Euclid when he was still a cop. He was smitten, so he stopped the Phantom Rental, parked at the curb and followed her on foot.

Connie was a shopper. She darted in and out of Euclid shops, and then walked north to Maryland Plaza. In those expensive shops Connie took her time. Milton would watch her from the sidewalk in the big picture windows of the shops. She bought anything she wanted, money was not a problem for her.

But Milton didn't know exactly where she lived. He had

become cautious toward the end of his Phantom Rapist career, and he would lay back as he followed Connie around the CWE.

He thought she lived on Buckingham Court, and he thought he knew which building she lived in but he wasn't certain, or what the address might be. He walked up and down Buckingham Court trying to get a feel for the apartment buildings, then went to the building he thought she lived in.

The glitzy apartments on Buckingham were different than the Washington University student apartments on Pershing or other streets in the West End. These buildings had secured entry doors leading into the apartments. And they had thick concrete walls so the residents wouldn't bother each other with loud conversations, televisions, or sex.

The locks on the secure doors were expensive, but would not be difficult to "jimmy" or pick if the burglar knew what he was doing. The residents would be wary of any stranger lurking on the street waiting for a chance to duck in with them while they were trying to get in with arms full of groceries. Milton read the names on the mailboxes in front of the apartment house. One jumped out at him, Miss Connie Rosenbaum.

Milton did a background check on Connie while he was still an active duty cop, by using the Haines directory in the Carondelet district detective bureau. It told him everything he needed to know about her. He pondered Connie Rosenbaum's future rape by him. He made plans and he was waiting for the right time to execute them.

On this fine summer day, Milton was parked at the curb in his dad's Oldsmobile 88. He was ogling the beautiful "hippie" girl who was hitchhiking on South Kingshighway at Arsenal, south of the CWE by about two miles.

Milton drove past her, observed her, and then turned around to watch her as she hitchhiked. He parked and stared as car after car drove by her without picking her up.

Finally a clean and new VW bug stopped for her. Milton got excited, it was another young woman who had stopped. The VW took off with Milton's dream girl and Milton followed the VW.

Milton got close to the VW then, drove in the left lane to gawk at the woman driving the Bug. It was his other heart throb, Connie Rosenbaum.

Milton followed them. Connie drove the "hippie" girl to Euclid and West Pine and dropped her off. The "hippie" girl ducked into a restaurant on the corner. Connie drove to Buckingham Court, parked at the curb and walked into the apartment at 4924 Buckingham Court.

Milton had enough information to execute his plans, but he decided to wait. What if the "hippie" girl and the classy news reporter were friends? If Milton could get them together in Connie's apartment, he could rape both of them.

Milton had nothing but time. He did a daily surveillance on Connie and the "hippie" girl. He followed Connie to work, watched her as she parked her shiny new bug in the Post-Dispatch employee parking area. He learned her schedule and watched her apartment.

The "hippie" girl came to visit Connie at her plush apartment frequently. Milton saw her, and he figured she lived somewhere on West Pine but he wasn't certain exactly where.

He checked the mail in the mailboxes for names of residents. Nothing "rang" for him. Since she didn't have a car, it was difficult to pinpoint her domicile.

But Milton still observed her walking, hitchhiking, and going into businesses on Euclid. Milton daydreamed about her and why she appealed to him. He figured it out: she was confident, like him. She walked with confidence. People with confidence have confident body language. It is what gets them through life.

    Maybe that's what attracted Connie to the "hippie" girl. They were as different as night and day. Connie had lived the life of a debutante. She went to the finest schools, and ultimately went to an ivy-league college.

    The "hippie" girl wanted to be an artist---but she knew nothing about art, its history or its famous painters. Those are basic knowledge skills for educated people. Art appreciation is an elective in every college in the United States.

    Connie mesmerized the "hippie" girl with her refinement. She advised her on educational opportunities, gave her art history books to read, and she cooked for her. Connie made sure the wandering "hippie" was fed, clean and safe. She had no idea that the Phantom Rapist had other plans for both of them.

17

On June 29, at about 4:00 P.M. Milton was on surveillance at West Pine and Euclid, parked at the curb in his dad's Oldsmobile. The street was bustling with activity, there were businesses on all four corners, and the huge Forest Park Hotel was the focal point of the intersection.

The "hippie" girl walked right past him, turned south on Euclid and crossed over to the west side of the street. Milton got out of his car and followed her on foot. She turned on Buckingham Court and walked directly to 4924.

Milton watched as the outer security door was "buzzed" open for her. His quarry was cornered, and it was time for Milton to strike. He paced himself, walking back and forth from Euclid to Buckingham Court devising his plan of attack.

He had made a closer inspection of the outside door, and he felt he could gain entry by using a credit card to slip the lock. It was not a big deal for him, or any other cop or burglar. It was like a jockey knowing when to whip his horse, or a race driver knowing when to down shift.

Milton made a quick look around the entry of the building. There was no one coming or going---he made his move. He quickly walked to the front security door, slipped a credit card between the lock and the jam, and he was inside.

Connie lived on the third floor. He took the stairs, and confidently walked to her door. He knocked. "Who is it?" Connie asked.

"Package for Miss Connie Rosenbaum," Milton loudly replied. Connie opened the door. Milton burst in with his revolver pointing at them. He was dressed in a white "T" shirt, was wearing gloves, a dark brimmed hat, and had on dark sunglasses.

"Don't look at me," he ordered them, "Look at the floor, or close your eyes," he continued. "I'm gonna fuck both of you bitches, get against the wall and turn your backs to me." The girls obeyed his commands. He had his knife on the "hippie" girl's neck, "Close those blinds or I cut the girl," he ordered Connie. Connie complied. Milton turned on the television and turned up the volume. He cut a cord from a hair dryer and tied Connie's wrists in front.

"If you do what I say, I won't kill you," Milton continued. He began cutting their clothing off of them with his knife, from the rear, tore at their clothing, and pushed them into the bedroom, then said, "Take the rest of your damned clothes off and get on that bed." The girls took their clothing off.

"Now, get on that bed and lay side by side," Milton ordered.

The girls complied.

The "hippie" girl mentally took herself to another place. She was going to go with the flow and move out of her body and into a spiritual condition. It was her way of survival.

Milton removed his trousers, then blindfolded the "hippie" girl with nylon stockings. He was trying to enter into the "hippie" girl when Connie intervened.

"Leave her alone, you bastard," Connie shouted, "She's just a kid."

Milton turned his rape intentions toward Connie Rosenbaum. It was tortuous for the "hippie" girl to lay next to Connie, nude, with the animal Milton Brookins in bed with them.

She wasn't sure what Milton was doing to Connie, but Connie was pleading with him, "Please don't do this, please I'm begging you not to do this." Sex with a man was an unnatural event for Connie.

Connie had had enough. She began fighting with Milton,

kicking and punching with her tied hands, and trying to get out of bed and run for help. The cord on her wrists became loose. Milton was trying to control her, trying to re-tie her wrists with the electrical cord.

The "hippie" girl pushed her blindfold away and watched as Milton began beating Connie with the pistol he had in his hand.

"You filthy rich white bitch," Milton said to her, "I'm in control here, you better give up that pussy or I'll kill both of you." Connie continued to struggle with him. The "hippie" girl jumped off of the bed. Milton was still beating Connie with the pistol.

Milton could see that he was losing control of the extravagant sex scene he had planned for himself.

Milton shot Connie Rosenbaum in the face with his revolver. The rape attempt was over. Milton quickly pulled on his trousers, took $24.00 from Connie's purse, and a ring from her finger, and ran from the apartment. He ran out of the front door of the building, and briskly walked to his dad's Oldsmobile at Euclid and West Pine. He drove directly to his home in Laclede Town.

Harry Glass, a maintenance man at the apartment building heard a scream and then a shot. He observed Milton running from the apartment. He followed him to Euclid and West Pine, and observed him get into his dads Olds.

The police were called. A ninth district detective bureau detective also responded. Detective Bill Miller had been in the ninth district for his entire career, and had been a detective for most of that time. He was in possession of photos of area rapists, and one of Milton Brookins.

The maintenance man, Harry Glass identified the photo of Milton Brookins as the assailant. Two women residing in the building also identified the photo of Milton Brookins.

"He was driving a real clean older model Oldsmobile 88,

dark top and bottom," Harry Glass stated.

Detective Bill Miller proceeded to Milton Brookins home in Laclede Town. He had four cops backing him up. He knocked on the door of the town home, and Cecelia, Milton's wife, answered the door. "Were looking for Milton," Detective Miller advised her.

"He's taking a bath," she informed the detectives. She went to the bathroom door and called out to Milton, "There's some detectives here to see you."

"I'm taking a bath," he shouted from the bathroom. "I'll be right out."

The detectives patiently waited. Milton came out of the bathroom dressed in a shirt and trousers. Detective Bill Miller placed handcuffs on him and told him he was under arrest for attempted rape and robbery.

Milton offered no resistance. He was placed in the backseat of the detective car and taken directly to Barnes Hospital. Other detectives went to the police department holdover and gathered up four more suspects who resembled Milton Brookins. They met Detective Bill Miller at Barnes.

Connie Rosenbaum was being treated for a bullet wound to her face. The physician treating her allowed the detectives to escort Milton Brookins and the other four men into her hospital room.

The men each were instructed to say things like, "Do as I say and I won't kill you."

Milton was instructed to put on the cracked sun glasses that were worn by Connie's and the "hippie" girl's assailant. The lens was cracked during the struggle with Connie.

Connie pointed at Milton Brookins, "That's him," Connie loudly said. "That's the man who forced his way into my apartment and tried to rape me. He tried to rape my friend, too. He shot me in the face, and he stole my ring and $24.00 from me."

Milton made no statement. He was conveyed to the ninth district station and booked for the attempted rape and shooting of Connie Rosenbaum, and assault with the intent to ravage the "hippie" girl, and the robbery of Connie Rosenbaum.

He was transferred to the downtown holdover. Warrants were applied for by Detective Bill Miller, and they were issued by the circuit attorney's office.

Milton was subsequently transferred to the dungeon-like St. Louis City Jail, the same jail Isom Combs Jr. was beaten and starved in.

His lawyer, Dan Reardon, requested a bond hearing for Milton. At the hearing, Judge David W. Fitzgibbons denied a bond for Milton Brookins, which can be done in a capital offense. He was to languish in the city jail until his trial.

18

The long process of prosecuting Milton Brookins had begun. Milton had cash, and cash is what Barrister Dan Reardon desired. The defense fund for Milton Brookins started by and funded by the black community, had grown. Most of the blacks did not believe Milton had committed the rapes.

Black men had been accused of and incarcerated for rapes of white women, and other trumped up charges, for a hundred years. Milton said he was innocent, that was enough for the blacks.

But the tide was turning for Milton Brookins, there was evidence left at the scene, evidence that indicated that he was there at Connie Rosenbaum's apartment on the day of the shooting, attempted rape, and robbery. Milton had transported his disguise, a hat, a pair of gloves, and a large pair of sunglasses, in a paper bag.

Before knocking on Connie's door, he retrieved the hat, the tight fitting leather gloves, and the sun glasses out of the paper bag, put them on his body, and tossed the paper bag under a table in the hallway of the apartment building.

His palm print was on the bag. The two residents of the apartment building who observed Milton told the investigating officers that Milton had been carrying a paper bag. They led the officers to the bag lying under the hallway table.

The bag was packaged and sent to the department crime lab. A police department fingerprint technician retrieved Milton's palm print from the bag.

The rumble in the black community, led by Barrister Dan Reardon, was that the St. Louis Police tricked Milton into holding the bag, then planted the bag at the scene.

That explanation was good enough for the black

community and the cash kept coming into the Milton Brookins defense fund at Gateway National Bank. That meant a big payday for Dan Reardon.

Milton's trial for the incident at 4924 Buckingham Court began on December 17 in the court of Circuit Judge Alan J. McFarland. He instructed the jury, and the trial began.
The Circuit Attorney's office hired Buzz Fredericks, a special assistant, to prosecute the case. After his opening statement to the jury, which consisted of ten men and two women, all white, Circuit Attorney Fredericks called Connie Rosenbaum to the stand.
Connie walked to the stand, was sworn in and took her seat. She wasn't dressed extravagantly, she wore plaid, in a business sort of way. She wore no gaudy jewelry, her hair was short and neat and freshly cut, and her makeup was sparse.
The members of the jury stared at her intently, dissecting her, trying to get a feel for her, wondering if they could believe her, deciding if they liked this reporter for the liberal newspaper, the lady of born-wealth, this person who said a suspended St. Louis Metropolitan Police Officer burst into her apartment and tried to rape her.
It was a crucial time in the trial, the defense studied the jurors, individually as they studied Connie Rosenbaum. Barrister Dan Reardon had questions he was asking to himself: Will she connect? How can I attack her and her story? I have to place a doubt in the jurors' minds. How can I do that? The witness is smart, educated, refined, where is the weakness?
There was no weakness in Connie Rosenbaum. She wore the scar on her face from Milton Brookins' bullet as a badge of courage. She spoke directly and answered the questions Buzz Fredericks asked her. It was time for her to tell her

story to the jurors.

"Tell the jury exactly what transpired on the afternoon that you and your house guest were attacked inside of your apartment at 4924 Buckingham Court."

Connie didn't clear her throat, she didn't start her story by saying "Well," she looked directly toward the jury box, and began.

"My guest and I were sitting on the floor, looking at some photographs that I had taken on a trip I had just gotten back from. There was a knock on the door. I asked who was there, and a voice said, "Package for Miss Connie Rosenbaum. I opened the door. A black man rushed into my apartment. He had a gun and a knife. He placed the knife at the neck of my guest, and he ordered me to close the blinds on the windows. He told us he was going to rape us. He turned the volume up on the television. He told us not to look at him, but we saw him anyway. He cut a cord from a hair dryer and was tying my hands with the cord. He told us he would kill us if we didn't do what he told us to do. He pushed us back into the bedroom, and ordered us to remove our clothing. He cut at our clothing with the knife, and then started ripping it off of us. We removed what he didn't cut off. He ordered me to get on the bed, on my back. I did as he said. He ordered my guest to kneel at the side of the bed. She did. He began to sexually fondle me, and I begged him to stop. He then ordered my guest to get on the bed beside me. He blindfolded her. After she got on the bed, he tried to rape her. I told him to leave her alone. She was just a kid. He turned his attention back to me. He tried to rape me, and I began fighting him. He beat me with his pistol, on the head and on my face. I still fought with him trying to get off of the bed. He shot me in the face with the pistol. I screamed, and he pulled on his trousers and fled from my apartment."

"Did he steal anything from you?" Buzz Fredericks

asked.

"Yes, he stole $24.00 that I had in my purse, and he stole a ring I was wearing," Connie replied.

"What did you do after he left your apartment?" Buzz Fredericks asked.

I opened the door of my apartment and screamed, then I called the police. I had gotten a towel from the bathroom and I compressed it on my face to try and stop the bleeding. The police came, and I was conveyed to Barnes Hospital."

"Is the man who burst into your apartment, attempted to rape and ravage you and your house guest, and shot you in the face present in the courtroom this morning?" Buzz Fredericks asked.

"Yes," Connie replied.

"Would you point him out for the jury?" Buzz Fredericks asked.

Milton had changed his appearance while languishing in the city jail. He now had a large mustache that covered his lower face, and he had a huge Afro style haircut.

Connie pointed directly at Milton Brookins---"The man sitting at the defense table wearing a brown suit," she stated.

"I have no further questions for Miss Rosenbaum, your honor," Buzz Fredericks said to the judge.

There was a brief recess, and then the beautiful "hippie girl" was called as a witness.

Buzz Fredericks asked her the same batch of questions. She gave her rendition of what occurred on the day of the shooting, ravaging and robbing. It was almost identical to Connie's statement.

There were cops called to testify. A fingerprint man from the laboratory testified to the paper bag and the palm print obtained from it belonging to Milton Brookins.

Detective Bill Miller, the detective who arrested Milton at his home on Red Maple Walk, testified to his participation in the arrest of Milton Brookins, and the show-up that was initiated at Connie Rosenbaum's hospital room.

Recess was called for the day. The jury was sequestered, and the judge desired that the trial resume early on the next day.

Milton Brookins took the stand in his own defense. He testified that he did not commit the robbery or the attempted rape, and that the first time he saw Connie Rosenbaum was at the hospital when he was placed in a show-up with four other men. He stated that he was out getting his car washed, came home at about 3:30, and walked to the Laclede Town swimming pool.

Milton's wife, Cecilia, testified that Milton was at home at the time of the incident.

The jury received instructions from Judge McFarland and retired at 5:50 P.M. to consider a verdict.

The jury convened for one hour and returned to the courtroom. They found Milton guilty on all counts.

Cecelia Brookins broke into tears. Milton looked at his wife and relatives as he was being led away. He was subsequently sentenced to 60 years on the shooting and robbery charge of victim Connie Rosenbaum, and 90 years for the attempted ravaging of the beautiful "hippie" girl. He was incarcerated in the Missouri State Penitentiary.

19

Apparently the Circuit Attorney's office made a decision not to prosecute Milton on the forcible rapes. The grand jury had indicted him on only two of the eighteen rapes.

The cases never went to trial. Detectives George Hotsenpiller and Bobby Matthews did not have their day in court testifying against Patrolman Milton Brookins.

The decision made sense. Why spend the state's money and put the victims through a trial if it was not necessary?

The trial would have been grueling for the victims. Their identities would have been known. Dan Reardon would have grilled them, and humiliated them on the witness stand.

In their minds, the sixty year sentence he received for the robbery and shooting of Connie Rosenbaum, and the ninety year sentence he received from the attempt to ravage the beautiful "hippie" girl were enough.

In essence, Milton got away with eighteen cases of forcible rape, and robbery. He boasted in his letters to the police that he raped over fifty women in the CWE and the West End of the City of St. Louis. He didn't serve any prison time for any of them.

It was as if the rapes and robberies never occurred. The victims try to forget. They want to put the horror of the incident behind them. They try to dismiss it, like it was a bad dream, a nightmare that they woke up from and quickly forgot about.

It was as if Milton knew he would not be punished for his crimes. It was a game for him, a game where he would come out a winner, and his victims would be scarred for life.

There are some things in life a victim cannot forget. Maybe an armed robbery, or a burglary, or having your car stolen, but forcible rape is there in the victim's mind forever. It's a nightmare a victim cannot wake up from.

But the victims got on with their lives knowing that Milton Brookins, the Phantom Rapist was safely tucked away in the Missouri State Penitentiary. He would not victimize another woman in his lifetime.

In a perfect world, not one governed by the criminal justice system, the victims would be correct in their assumption that Milton would never again be free.

But there is no perfection in the criminal justice system. The phrase "criminal justice" is an oxymoron, and the people who believe in it are morons.

There was still defense fund cash in the Gateway National Bank. Appeals are expensive, sometimes in the six figure range. Barrister Dan Reardon wasn't about to turn his back on his client Milton Brookins.

During Milton's first trial, the lady who guided the investigating officers (Mrs. Nancy Tresslar) to the paper bag under a table in the Buckingham Court apartment hallway gave a sworn deposition to the circuit attorney's office.

She had been preparing to leave St. Louis for the Great State of Texas. She moved before the first trial. Dan Reardon sought a retrial on the grounds that Milton's constitutional rights were violated because he was denied access to a witness, and was not given the opportunity to confront the witness in a court of law.

The appeal also stated that the jury was tainted by news articles mentioning Milton Brookins' name, and identifying him as the Phantom Rapist who had raped and robbed eighteen women in the CWE and the West End.

The Missouri Supreme Court granted Milton a new trial. Connie Rosenbaum and the beautiful "hippie" girl had to testify again.

Milton's new trial was scheduled for August of 1972, and then postponed. The witness who observed the paper bag had to be summoned from Texas. The trial began in October of 1972.

A jury of eleven men and one woman heard testimony in the court of Ivan Lee Holt Jr. The jury deliberated for less than two hours, and found Milton guilty. He was given a life sentence.

20

Most of Milton Brookins' victims scattered for parts unknown. It is one of the perks of living in a free society. It's a big country. A victimized person can go north, south, east, or west. It is everyone's dream to reinvent oneself. Few people do it.

Personal reinvention is spurred by a negative action. Usually it's a failed marriage or love affair, or a career failure.

Most of us stay where we feel home is. Many people who go away from home to attend college feel their college home is the place where they belong.

People who come to St. Louis to attend college usually leave immediately after graduation. The west coast is a big draw for St. Louis folk.

Connie Rosenbaum stayed in the Central West End. St. Louis was her power base. Her dad was prominent and wealthy. But her scars were deeper than the bullet wound scar given to her by the Phantom Rapist, Patrolman Milton Brookins.

She got back into the routine of news reporting for the liberal St. Louis Post-Dispatch. Living and working in St. Louis was her life, her reason for existing, it was home to her.

Her friends and relatives saw a change in her, she escaped into her own world, and nobody could reach her to drag her back to the real world.

The beautiful "hippie" girl stayed in her carriage house and flourished in the Central West End. She continued her existence by working in the art world. She started attending classes at Forest Park College, just a stone's throw from the CWE.

She worked at being an artist, and the career eventually worked for her. While attending college she met another artist, and they worked together on several art projects. They married, and the beautiful "hippie" girl now lives in a mansion in the West End.

Her paintings and her husband's art work adorn the walls, and they display their pottery and sculptures on shelves and stands in the large house. They travel and are hired by colleges and universities to supervise archeological digs.

She has a master of fine arts degree from Fontbonne College, where she majored in interior design and piano. She is still mentally scarred by the thought of the Phantom Rapist, Milton Brookins. She owns two huge German Shepherd attack dogs. They wander the house at will.

Shortly after Milton Brookins was found guilty of attempting to ravage her and given a life sentence, the beautiful "hippie" girl received an anonymous telephone call. "We're going to get you, girl," the voice said.

She believed the caller, and she has taken precautions for her entire life. Her encounter with Milton Brookins was a master's degree in street smarts. Never trust a stranger----never open your door for anybody you do not know.

Patrolman Ron Adler's plan for upward mobility in the St. Louis Metropolitan Police Department paid off. He was transferred to the prestigious Special Operations Deployment Division, under the command of Chief of Detectives, Lieutenant Colonel John Doherty.

The years quickly clicked by for Ron Adler. He was promoted to sergeant, and after a short stint in the bloody ninth district in uniform, he was transferred back to the Bureau of Investigation, again working for Colonel Doherty.

John Doherty was approaching mandatory retirement age. When a cop demigod leaves the bureaucracy his personal staff are "up for grabs" within the department. Most go back to a district in uniform and work the trenches, something they are not accustomed to and are not willing to do.

John Doherty warned his most trusted sycophants----"Find a home fast, I'll be leaving soon."

Ron Adler was a lucky guy. John Doherty's retirement fell near Ron's twenty year anniversary in the department. The twenty year mark is like an insurance policy being paid up for life, one the insured can collect from for the rest of his or her life.

The problem with the police department pension system evolves around the police officer's marital status. If a copper is divorced, part of his pension goes to the divorced spouse.

Ron had met a younger woman, and felt this woman was the love of his life. He was newly divorced, and searching for a place to roost.

Ron retired from the department with 40% of his base pay, which wasn't much in 1980. He landed a security director's job for a retail store in the area. He worked there for a while then landed a good job with one of John Doherty's most trusted and revered friends, power broker Gene Slay.

Gene Slay was a man's man, which is why he and John Doherty were friends. Gene took his dad's small trucking company in south St. Louis and built it into an empire.

He became friends with congressmen, senators and presidents. His brother, Hank Slay, was closely associated with Matthew Trupiano, the reputed head of the St. Louis Mafia.

Gene Slay was close to Sorkis Webbe Sr., who was indicted along with Matthew Trupiano for attempting to be paid for cable television coming into the St. Louis area.

Gene Slay had always had John Doherty as his head of

security. That meant Lieutenant Colonel John Doherty, Chief of Detectives for the St. Louis Metropolitan Police Department, was the bodyguard for Gene Slay. John Doherty did Gene Slay's duty.

Gene Slay had enemies, thug enemies. The union thugs feared Chief of Detectives John Doherty, and so did the St. Louis and Chicago Mafia. Lieutenant Colonel John Doherty's army of cops was bigger than the Mafia's army of thugs, and more adept at killing.

If organized criminals messed with Gene Slay, Chief of Detectives John Doherty would come down on them like a battalion of Force-Recon Marines.

But when Lieutenant Colonel John Doherty retired, he could no longer bodyguard for Gene Slay. He didn't have his army of willing cops to do his will.

John Doherty took a job with Anheuser Busch--- he was big-friends with the Busch family also. He sat in an office with a view of South Broadway and shuffled papers for a living.

Businessmen like Gene Slay needed employees they could trust. Gene direly needed a bodyguard---he also was an old man with a reputation that needed to be guarded. John Doherty vouched for Ron Adler, and Ron hit the ground running for Gene Slay. Ron was Gene Slay's bodyguard and shadow for 20 years.

Ron worked for Slay Trucking Company until Gene Slay died. He lives in St. Charles County with his wife, and is semi-retired. Ron and his wife own payday loan companies in the St. Charles County area.

Ron is now a businessman----no more toiling for peanuts and doing favors for a transfer to a soft clothes job. Ron was in the game for the cash, and he was reaping the benefits of high interest loans.

But there was a glitch in the money making plans of Ron

Adler; he became ill, unable to maintain his business interest, unable to walk without falling. His young wife took over the responsibility of their lucrative loan business. Ron telephones me occasionally, he can hardly speak, and when he does he is difficult to understand. It's as if it is written in the scriptures, "Old cops shalt not enjoy wealth."

Sammy Lackland, Ron Adler's laid-back partner in the Wild West seventh district, was also moved to a downtown detective bureau. He was promoted a couple of times, achieved the rank of Lieutenant, retired, and after several years of retirement, died at a young age.

Detective George Hotsenpiller was involved in a serious auto accident in the seventh district while on-duty. His shoulder and knee were damaged beyond repair, and he was placed on light-duty.

He was moved to prisoner processing, booking prisoners at the downtown holdover. The department physician, Dr. James F. Cooper, recommended that he be given a disability pension.

George languished in prisoner processing, booking prisoners, for months awaiting his pension. His buddy and partner, Detective Bobby Mathews visited him frequently.

There are certain things that are sacred in the cop business. The most sacred is the bond between 2 cops who work well together.

A good partnership in a cop car, or when interviewing victims or suspects is priceless. It's like a painting by Picasso---once it's destroyed, it's gone forever.

Bobby Matthews knew he would never enjoy the job again without George Hotsenpiller as his partner.

Bobby Matthews had gone through a divorce, and he was floundering within the police department like a salmon trying to swim upstream.

Bobby Matthews always seemed to be in the wrong place

at the wrong time. George Hotsenpiller managed to keep Bobby safe and out of trouble during their tenure as partners, but as soon as Bobby got on his own, the bottom fell out for him.

Bobby was off-duty and in the 500 block of Rosedale, in the heart of the Wild West seventh district, late at night. No one knows exactly why he was there, alone on the street, and Bobby wasn't giving the reason.

Bobby was accosted by two street robbers at approximately 1:00 A.M. They got the drop on Bobby (one of them had a sawed off shotgun) and forced him into an alley. They took Bobby's wallet, which contained $21.00, and were walking away when one of the robbers opened Bobby's wallet and observed his police badge.

The robber with the wallet shouted, "Hey, he's a damned cop."

The robber with a sawed-off shotgun whirled and fired at Bobby with both barrels. Bobby had already ducked behind a tree and as the robbers were running down the alley, Bobby fired at them with his 38 snub nosed revolver.

Bobby chased the bandits, firing at them until his gun was empty. They got away with his badge and wallet. Bobby felt on his body for signs of warm red liquid. He was lucky, he wasn't shot. But he did some soul searching. Every cop does at some point in his cop career. Bobby talked to his new wife about a possible lifestyle change.

George Hotsenpiller was going to be pensioned out of the police department. There wasn't any other cop he wished to have as a partner. Bobby's wife had a nest egg. They both figured it was time for Bobby to explore new horizons.

Having grown up on a prison farm, viewing prisoners and prison guards for as long as he could remember, and hearing prison tales from his dad, Bobby felt he had been in law enforcement for his entire life.

Both Bobby Matthews and George Hotsenpiller had seventeen years on the department. Bobby visited George at prisoner processing. He advised George that he was leaving the department. He and his new wife had purchased a fish camp at Lake Wappepello in downstate Missouri.

He was going to be a fishing guide, rent cabins, fishing boats, and just sit back and rake in the money. George envied Bobby for his courage; it was a long shot, but George figured Bobby might make it as a guide.

There are "turnkeys" who work in prisoner processing. They aren't police officers, although they wear the same uniform, and are armed with the same sidearm as cops.

Their badges are different, and their pay isn't as much as a city cop. They are employees of the city police department who do menial jobs, such as transporting prisoners and housing prisoners in the temporary jail cells until they are either released or transferred to the city jail.

Turnkeys work at the same job for most of their careers and every cop who makes arrests knows who they are, and is friends with them.

When Bobby Matthews came to prisoner processing to say his goodbyes to George and the staff at prisoner processing, an old black "turnkey" listened intently to Bobby's farewell.

The old "turnkey" felt sad that Bobby was leaving, and he could read George's remorse that he was losing his partner and friend.

"Do y'all allow any Negroes down there at that lake?" the "turnkey" asked.

Bobby paused before answering, and glanced at George, "Oh, yeah, we can always use some bait." Bobby walked out amidst loud laughter.

On September 30, 1974, Connie Rosenbaum hanged

herself in her apartment at 4927 Laclede, just one short block from her previous apartment on Buckingham Court.

Her mother had responded to Connie's apartment after she could not get in touch with her by telephone.

She used a key to gain entry, and after searching the apartment she found Connie hanging in a hallway closet. She was last seen riding her bicycle in Forest Park on the previous day. Connie Rosenbaum did not leave a suicide note.

In October of 1975 George Hotsenpiller's disability retirement was granted to him. He was a likeable guy, and he landed a job with a utility company in the city. He stayed there and got a good retirement from them. George lived a good life. He now lives in a rural part of outstate Missouri.

Bobby Matthews lived the life of a fishing guide, got divorced again, found a woman who would take care of him, and married for a third time. He died three years ago.

Milton Brookins was released from prison in September of 2006. He spent thirty seven years in the Missouri State Penitentiary. He took an apartment at 5622 Enright, in the West End, in the neighborhood of his previous rapes.

Ironically, the beautiful "hippie" girl lives her life of serendipity just 2 blocks from where Milton took up residence. She may have passed him on the street. I'm, certain she would not recognize him, but he would recognize her.

Milton Brookins, phantom, burglar, rapist, robber, liar and St. Louis police officer, died at the age of sixty nine, on November 2, 2010.

21

Serial rapist Milton Brookins was out of commission forever, but the rapes did not stop on or near the Washington University Campus. Raping was the culture of the sub-culture. In 1970 there were five forcible rapes at Washington University. In 1971 there were nine.

The hierarchy of the St. Louis Metropolitan Police Department were embarrassed by the actions of one of their own, Patrolman Milton Brookins. They were also humiliated by the insurmountable unsolved rapes still occurring in the West End, and near the Washington University Campus.

On October 19, 1971, two female medical students were walking in the 6100 block of Pershing. Two people approached them from the rear. One of them stuck something hard in the victim's back, the second assailant waved a broken soda bottle in the face of the other victim and got her in a strangle hold.

The street predators told them to continue walking until they got to a vacant house at 6141 Pershing. One victim broke away and ran, screaming for help in the darkness. The other victim was taken into the basement of the vacant house. Residents heard the screams and called the police.

The victim said she was told to disrobe after entering the basement but she refused. She was told she would be killed if she did not disrobe, so she removed her pants and panties. She was raped at that time.

A young police officer, James Perrot, was dispatched to the scene. Officer Perrot went to the rear of the building with a flashlight and observed women's undergarments in a passageway lying on the floor. He followed the passageway to a room where the rapist and the victim were lying on the floor.

The rapist jumped up and grabbed the victim's hair, "Get away or I'll kill her," he shouted. The rapist made a move toward his waist band as if he was going for a weapon and Officer Perrot shot one time. The bullet hit the rapist in the forehead. He died a couple of hours later at Homer G. Phillips Hospital.

The victim got up and dressed. She looked at Officer Perrot and said, "You didn't have to kill him." The rapist was identified as 16 year old Frederick Lamont Minor.

Officer Jim Perrot was awarded the department's highest award, The Medal of Valor. Several years later he resigned from the police department to become a security guard at Anheuser Busch, every St. Louis cop's dream job.

The rapes would slow for a while, then an unwary student would let her guard down, walk at night, ride her bicycle in the dark, or allow a stranger to enter her apartment to use the telephone. The rapists were always watching and waiting.

The culture of Mill Creek Valley was moving north to North St. Louis County. There were apartments there with section 8 housing. Thousands of black city-dwellers flocked to Spanish Lake and took up residence in once ritzy apartment complexes with indoor swimming pools, workout rooms, and glamorous apartments.

The children of the residents of North County were naive. They had lived a safe and stable life in the little berg of Spanish Lake. "Love thy neighbor as thy self," was their mantra.

At the eastern edge of Spanish Lake is the Mississippi River, close to the confluence of the Mississippi and Missouri Rivers. The water is unforgiving there, where the rivers join there is turbulence for miles southward past the City of St. Louis.

The Chain of Rocks Bridge, which connects Missouri

with Illinois, was closed after fifty years of service. There were barricades on both sides of the river and "no trespassing" signs.

    Julie and Robin Kerry, sisters and teenagers, frequented the Chain of Rocks Bridge. It was a hangout for Spanish Lake kids. A hole in the chain link fence allowed entry to a place where teenagers could get away from authority and enjoy the view of the confluence of the Missouri and Mississippi.

    Julie wrote poems about togetherness, friendship, equality, peace and love among the other graffiti on the bridge deck.

    A cousin, Thomas Cummins, was in town from the south and the Kerry sisters wanted to show him the bridge and Julie's philosophical graffiti.

    It was late on April 4, 1991 when the three of them ventured onto the bridge span. Earlier in the evening, four other teenagers were drinking beer and smoking marijuana at one of their apartments in North County.

    Reginald Clemons, along with Marlin Gray, Daniel Winfrey, and Antonio Richardson, stoned and brainwashed teenagers, also decided to visit the bridge.

    They met up with the Kerry sisters and their cousin. There was some casual conversation, and the two groups passed each other. Clemons then made a suggestion, "Lets rob them."

    Marlon Grey replied, "Yeah, I feel like hurting somebody." Antonio Richardson suggested they rape the girls.

    As a group they headed back toward the Kerry sisters and their cousin, Thomas Cummins. They tore the clothing off of the Kerry sisters, beat them, and individually raped them. They tossed the Kerry sisters off of the bridge---the 70 foot fall to the Mississippi River was hardly survivable.

Thomas Cummins jumped. He saw Julie Kerry in the water and grabbed for her. They both went under, separated and Cummins surfaced to make his way to the Missouri river bank.

Julie Kerry's body was recovered days later in Caruthersville, Missouri. Robin's body was never recovered. City police were called after Cummins flagged down a car. City homicide handled the case.

The Kerry sisters were cute, petite teeny-boppers excited about life and the future. They had a lot to offer this world.

At face value, the cops suspected Cummins of murdering his cousins. He was intently interrogated, something no innocent person should be subjected to, but cops see things blankly until little pieces of convoluted fact enter into their psyche.

The little false facts form a story in the cop's brain, and the cop believes it as the gospel. The cops hammer and interrogate until they get what they want from the suspect/victim. Thomas Cummins was not a worldly guy— he was vulnerable, but he stuck to his story and took the abuse.

Finally, someone found a flashlight left at the scene. It had a name engraved on it, and it led to the suspects.

Daniel Winfrey, who was 15 at the time, was sentenced to 30 years in prison. Reginald Clemons and Marlon Gray were sentenced to death. Antonio Richardson was sentenced to death, but it was overturned to life in prison.

The rapes in the West End of the City of St. Louis had slowed, and the coeds of Washington University became lax in their self-protection.

On May 5th, 1995, Melissa Gail Aptman, Washington University student and a coed friend, ate and drank at Chuey Arzola's Tex-Mex Restaurant in Dog Town, near the

Washington University Campus. It had the best Tex-Mex food in the region.

Melissa was not new to St. Louis. She was two weeks shy of graduation, she knew St. Louis streets were jungles with jackals lurking in every dark crevice waiting for prey to wander by.

But she and her friend were in Dogtown, a city neighborhood known for its bars, its St. Pats Parade, and Chuey's Tex-Mex Restaurant. Dogtown had always been safe.

Melissa was no country-bumpkin. She grew up in Miami, the daughter of a prominent neurosurgeon. She was smart, sophisticated and hip.

She had parked her car on Art Hill Place, a nifty clean street with neat houses, just a short distance from the restaurant. It was dark when they happily left the restaurant and slowly walked to her car.

Andre Bonds, twenty, and Bryan Cook, sixteen, were waiting at Melissa's Jeep Grand Cherokee for the young coeds. Andre Bonds had a 22 caliber pistol and he shoved it in the two victim's faces as he ordered them to get into the car and shut-up.

Melissa screamed for help. Andre Bonds shot her with his 22, and stuffed her into the Jeep. She died a slow death, the small, high velocity 22 caliber round bounces around inside of its victim, severing arteries and destroying organs.

They abducted the terrified coed friend, and drove the Jeep to East St. Louis, Illinois, beat, tortured and gang raped the friend, then Andre shot her with the 22.

Both of them were dumped onto an East St. Louis street and left for dead. The coed friend survived.

Andre Bonds was sentenced to death. Bryan Cook received six life terms.

Phantom Rapist 217

The rapes, the abductions and the murders of young women are still prevalent in St. Louis. It isn't a phenomenon started by Patrolman Milton Brookins.

Patrolman Billy Robinson, my Police Academy classmate, and my riding partner in the bloody ninth district, went through the rapes of Milton Brookins. Milton was Billy's associate, and Billy enjoyed speaking of him and his life of crime while hiding behind a St. Louis cop badge.

It's what cops do, we talk. Billy, a black St. Louis inner city cop, and me a white eastside ex-Marine, we asked each other the question that cops ask daily: Why did he do it?

Milton wasn't there to answer our question. He was rotting away in the Missouri State Penitentiary.

We came to a conclusion: Milton's crimes against young white women, and similar crimes initiated by other ghetto young men, are not crimes of sexual gratification, or monetary gain. The modus operandi is hatred!

One thing for certain: The coed rape victims, who weren't murdered, will never forget their college experience in good old St. Louis.

Cops are nosey creatures. We never forget a case, no matter how trivial, and we always feel the need to revisit old cases and verify in our little cop brains that everything turned out the way it was supposed to turn out.

City cops occasionally are required to go to the state penitentiary in Jefferson City, Missouri to interview prisoners.

A couple of years had passed since Milton Brookins had been sentenced to a life sentence in the state penitentiary. A couple of district detectives travelled to Jefferson City to interview a prisoner. The prison was dilapidated, akin to a Civil War prison, a human zoo. It was frightening to enter.

The cop detectives interviewed the prisoner and were

preparing to leave. One of them asked a guard supervisor about Milton Brookins.

He was advised that Milton had been beaten and raped as soon as he was placed into the prison population. He was turned into a "prison girl" and passed around as a sex slave.

As I have stated in this little book, justice is fleeting and in most cases nonexistent. The Babylonian King, Hammurabi, devised a code for the punishment of criminals. "Let the punishment fit the crime. An eye for an eye."

To the victims of Milton Brookins, those beautiful young women who were beaten, abused, humiliated, forced to cower in a corner, and raped: did Milton's punishment fit his crime?

As a cop, I offer you consolation, and I apologize to you for not warning you that cops cannot protect you. You must protect yourself. We arrive after the fact, and, to some extent, we feel we are important and that you as a victim are not important because in many instances, we feel you set yourself up to be a victim.

Patrolman Milton Brookins was placed in a dungeon and raped for 37 years. An eye for an eye!

"INDEX"

A

Adler, Ron (Detective Sergeant)52,53,55,58,102,103,119,169,173,175,182,204,205,206
Aiuppa, Joey Doves (organized criminal) 205
Agers, Donald--59
Altheimer, Ruth—217
Ashe, Arthur—15,16.

B

Baker, Josephine 9
Benson, Mike. (Patrolman)—58,59
Blancett, Chester (Sgt)—65,67,126,149,150,152,160,168,169,
Beene, Leamon--777
Berger, Jerome—15,16,22
Boone, Royce (Patrolman) 72
Bond, Leslie 13
Boston, Strangler 38
Brawley, Dennis 167
Brookins, Celia 37-199
Brookins, Milton—15,20,21,22,25,26,27,33,44,51,58,6671,75,77,83,84,88,8994,112,137,139,142,145,152,153,155,165,166,167,166,169 170,173,174,175,176,179,181,182,186,187,190,192,193,195,196,199,200201,202,210,211,216
Brostron, Curtis (Chief) 50
Brown, Cordell 138
Broughton, Bob (Patrolman) 91,92

Bruen, Robert 60

C

Clapton, Eric 13
Combs, Isom Jr. 155,156,157,158,166,167,175,176,177,178,181
Clay, William (Congressman) 11
Constant, Michael (Professor) 36
Corcoran, James (Circuit Attorney) 178, 179
Cox, William (Detective) 147
Curtis, Tony (Actor) 38

D

Daly, Tom (Patrolman) 138
Dietrich, Yevon (criminal) 55
Doherty, John (Colonel) 102,104,106,205,206
Downey, Bob (Detective) 147
Doyle, Ed 162, 163
Doyle's Phillip 68, 162
Drake, Charles 7,8
Dylewski, Stan 153

E

Egenreither, Ed (detective) 93
Ellis, Frank (Detective) 77
Elephant Lounge 126, 163
England, Larry 81

F

Fitzgerald, William (Sgt.) 82, 94, 95
Freeman, Harry (Acting Sergeant) 30, 31, 110, 111, 112, 171
Fredericks, Buzz 196,198

G

Gamble, Hamilton 7
Glass, Harry 192
Glasscock, Jim 82, 83
Grimes, Fred 94, 96

H

Hawkins, William (Detective) 78
Hindrichs, David (Patrolman) 65, 66, 67
Hippie Girl 184, 185, 186, 188, 189, 191, 192, 201, 203, 204, 210
Hotsenpiller, George (Detective) 50,51,126,127,130,132,133,135,139,141,144,149,150,151,158,159,160,161,164,175,182,200,207,208,209,210
Hutnick, Melroy (Assistant Circuit Attorney) 96, 97, 98, 100, 173

I

J

Jagger, Mick 14
Jinkerson, Larry (Detective) 68, 85, 87
Johnson, Myron 94, 95, 96, 97, 98

K

Kennedy, Arthur 177
Kirner, Dan 93
Kunstler, William 15

L

Lackland, Sam 52, 53, 58, 108, 169, 173, 182
Laclede Town 14, 31, 32
Lee, Harry 81,94,97
Letz, John Michael (Patrolman) 74
Liebsch, Larry 85
Lowell, David 77
Lynch, Jadwick (Detective) 77

M

Matthews, Bobby (Detective) 50,51,52,86,126,127,128,129,132,133,134,135,139,140,144, 149,150,151,158,159,160,161,164,167,170,171,172,175,182 ,299,207,208,209,210
McCahan, John 147
McCrary, Charles 86
Mill Creek Valley 8,17,18, 212
Miller, Bill, Detective 193,194

N

Northcutt, Dave, Patrolman 80

O

O'Connels Pub 95, 96, 98
Oitker, Gene (Detective) 147
Ornstein, J.M. (Dr.) 139
Otten, Walter (Patrolman) 70

P

Parton, Al, Sergeant 104
Patty, Jack, (cop) 555, 103
Perrot, James (Patrolman) 211
Pietrowski, William (Detective) 77
Pollock, Joe 15
Prinzen, Ray 72

Q

R

Reardon, Dan, (Lawyer) 174, 181, 199, 196, 201
Robinson, Joseph 85
Robinson, William (Patrolman) 39, 40, 216
Riley, William (prisoner) 179
Rosenbaum, Connie 186, 188, 189, 190, 191, 192, 193, 196, 201, 203, 209

S

Sanaamon, Detective 68, 85, 87
Saxon, Eddie 16

Seay, Norman 11
Slay, Eugene (Power broker) 205, 206
Skinner, Ralph (Sergeant) 161
Smith, Larry (Burglar) 104
Stern, Roy (Patrolman) 142
Swink, Donald (Prisoner) 179

T

Terry, Carl (Prisoner) 179
Tick Tock Club 175
Timmons, Prince (Patrolman) 76
Townsend, Dennis (Patrolman) 167
Tresslar, Nancy 201
Tucker, Gary (Patrolman) 163, 164, 168

V

Vasel, Pete 55, 103

W

Wachter, Tony (Detective) 82, 83, 94, 95, 96
Webb, Lula Mae 20, 39
West End 33, 38
Wideman, Dwight (Patrolman) 77, 81
Whitelaw (street) 161
Williams, Paul (Burglar) 104
Wood, Oliver (Patrolman) 139
Wood River, Il. 160